PRAISE FOR THE MARRIAGE ADVENTURE

"Marriages are never static. We are moving in a positive or negative direction. We are more likely to reach a positive destination if we know where we are going. In The Marriage Adventure, Daniel and Bonnie Hoover, offer practical steps in co-operating with God to clarify the purpose and mission of your marriage; thus making your marriage a positive, God honoring adventure."

GARY CHAPMAN, Ph.D.
Author of The 5 Love Languages

"Many times, in marriage, we settle for something far less than God originally indented. In The Marriage Adventure, Daniel & Bonnie Hoover share how intentionally living on mission can change not only the trajectory of your relationship with your spouse but your entire family."

MARK BATTERSON, New York Times
best-selling author of The Circle Maker
Lead Pastor of National Community Church

"I agree with the Hoovers that mission is the mainstay of a growing, intimate and spiritually alive marriage, and I'm pleased to see a well-written book hone in on this topic."

GARY THOMAS, Best-selling Author of
Sacred Marriage & When to Walk Away

"Merriam Webster defines "adventure" as 'the exploration of unknown territory.' Daniel & Bonnie Hoover's book, The Marriage Adventure, is the perfect trail map for married couples to explore and ultimately conquer marriage's 'unknown territory' and not only survive the adventure... but thrive. Great read! Great read!"

IRA BLUMENTHAL, Best-selling author, public speaker, founder of Co-Opportunities, Inc.

"When a person is heading out on an adventure into unknown territory, they are always looking for the best guides and maps available! I cannot think of any better guides than Daniel & Bonnie Hoover, they live out in their marriage everything they write about in their book! I have had a front row seat to watch them over the past 15 years and I am here to tell you that you can trust these guides and their map to a great marriage!"

MIKE LINCH, Senior Pastor NorthStar Church, Host of "Linch with a Leader" Podcast

THE MARRIAGE ADVENTURE

DISCOVERING MISSION FOR YOUR MARRIAGE

DANIEL & BONNIE HOOVER

XULON PRESS

Xulon Press
2301 Lucien Way #415
Maitland, FL 32751
407.339.4217
www.xulonpress.com

CONTENTS

To
Heyward and Jennie Hoover
Tot Free and the late Jim Free

Through highs, lows, and everything in between,
we are grateful for the examples you set for us
through your Marriage Adventures.
You have paved the way for a lasting legacy.

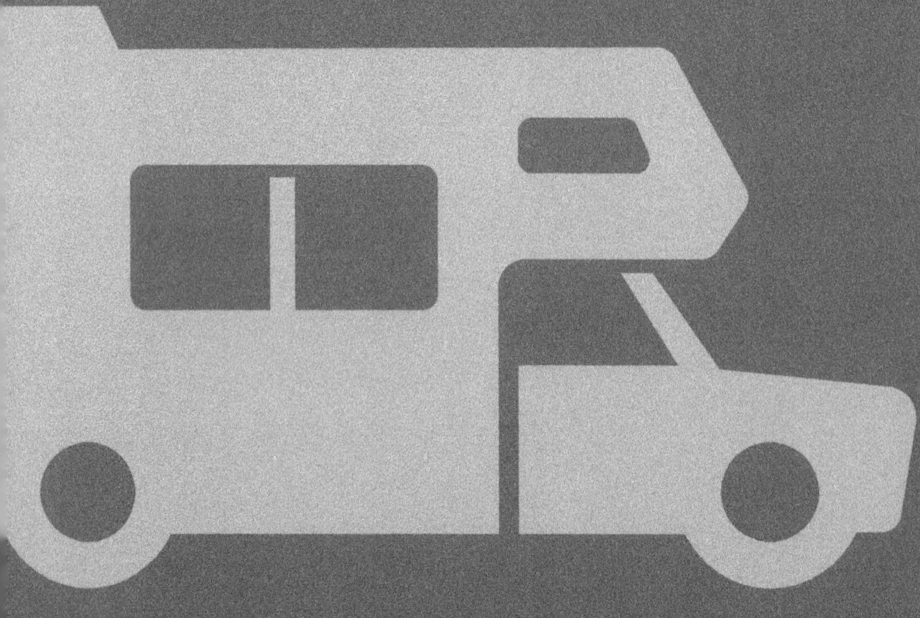

A NOTE FROM THE AUTHORS

Our family loves adventure! Whether it's camping, kayaking, paddle boarding, zip lining, or renovating a twenty-year-old motorhome together, we enjoy the thrill of a good challenge. Nothing is more challenging or adventurous than marriage, and that's what this book is all about.

Each chapter will take you along a leg of our two-week road trip to the Grand Canyon and Sedona with our eleven and nine-year-old children. We also intertwine stories from our twenty-five years of marriage. We assure you, neither have been perfect. But we've learned a lot along our journey and are still learning.

If you read a story about a couple and think we are writing about you, we probably are, and we probably are not! The truth is, we find ourselves in many of these examples, as well. Our pastor often says, "that which is most personal is most universal." Through our many years of workshops and counseling, we hear stories repeat themselves over and over. Just know that we have changed most names and some details to honor those we love and are traveling alongside on this marriage adventure. You are not alone, and your story is most likely someone else's.

We pray you will read this with an open heart toward the Lord and what He wants to do in your relationship with your spouse. No matter where you find yourself along the journey, it's easy to feel stuck in the mundane or what feels like wreckage on the side of a winding road. It's helpful to pull back and see that this is just one short leg of a lifelong adventure, where the journey itself is the destination.

After twenty-five years of marriage, we have found that we are starting to finish each other's sentences. That may be evident as you are reading and aren't sure which one of us is speaking. We've tried to denote with parentheses when the writer is unclear. If you aren't sure who is speaking, don't worry, you are still hearing from our united hearts.

We hope you enjoy our two-week family cross-country adventure. But more importantly, we pray you will discover the unique mission and grand plan God has for you in your own *Marriage Adventure*.

Daniel & Bonnie Hoover

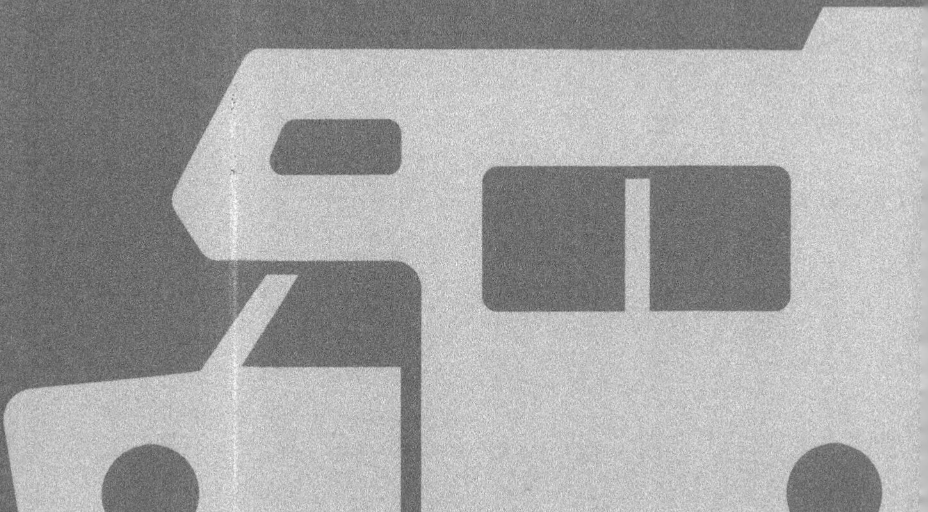

INTRODUCTION

"THIS IS NOT WHAT I SIGNED UP FOR"

A s I reached for another handgrip, I felt my feet slipping beneath me. Perched on a ledge high above Sedona's gorgeous red rock formations, Daniel could see the panic on my face. The only thing running through my mind was, *your kids need you to keep it together!* So, I told myself I wouldn't look down. Staring at the 4,500 feet of emptiness between me and the ground would not help me cope with my current situation.

I thought to myself, *why on Earth did we decide to climb Bell Rock with a nine and eleven-year-old?* An experienced climber might look around with pride at the accomplishment that had led her to this majestic view. But all I could see was fear in the faces of my children and imagined imminent tragedy.

Daniel had gone on a reconnaissance mission to find a safer passage down. I looked up at him biting back tears as he rounded the corner of the rock. He said, "Ok, I have good news and bad news. The good news, there is a way down. Bad news, we have to go down the way we came up!" Though I kept the words from escaping, inwardly, I was screaming; *this is NOT what I signed up for!*

A Couple in Crisis

"This is not what I signed up for!" Millie finally broke the silence between them through tears as they sat with a flat tire in the middle of nowhere, Kansas. "I just don't think I can make this work anymore."

I (Daniel) sat in my office listening to the couple explaining the moment they realized they needed to seek counseling for their broken marriage.

Matt recalled feeling stunned at the words he was hearing from his wife as he knelt to change the tire. He didn't know if she was referring to the massive cross-country trip they were on or their eight-year marriage. Communication had been strained and they hadn't been intimate for some time now. Things hadn't been perfect, but this? Had he heard her correctly? Matt reached back through nearly a decade of memories, arguments, and disappointments, searching for answers as to what might have led them here. This trip was supposed to be an adventure that would help their family reconnect and for he and Millie to rekindle their love for each other.

As giddy newlyweds, they had survived the first year of living on beans and rice in their one-bedroom apartment as they paid off the remainder of Millie's college debt. The upgrade to the three-bedroom house was a stretch, but they knew both of their salaries would handle the higher mortgage. Having been in their new home for ten months, they were surprised with a baby on the way.

Millie loved her job as a pediatric nurse, but they decided it would be better for her to stay home with their son, Ethan, when he was born. It wasn't ideal timing, but they thought they could make it work. Life at home with a baby wasn't the easiest for Millie. Though she was in love with her son, she wrestled with resentment for what this new arrangement had cost her.

Matt recalled his long days at the office, and the extra hours he had picked up on the weekends to allow Millie to stay home. Even though he was great at his job in sales, it felt like a tremendous sacrifice. He still gritted his teeth as he remembered walking in the door at the end of the day, exhausted from his second job. Millie would almost dump Ethan in his arms as she headed out for a night with some of her girlfriends, offering him barely more than the same instructions she would have given a hired sitter. He felt a bit used, even hurt, that she wasn't happy to see him. He didn't realize at the time that his heart had taken a few steps away from Millie in self-defense.

Before long, he started feeling a bit like an outsider. Unknowingly, Millie reinforced Matt's insecurities as a dad every time she corrected how he fed, bathed, dressed, or even played with Ethan. Because he felt appreciated and needed at work, he slipped into a habit of coming home later and later.

Matt remembered the growing coldness between him and Millie as Ethan's second birthday approached, which is why it shocked him when she announced she wanted them to have another baby. It felt like it was coming from "out of the blue," but he was willing to try. Maybe it would make things better.

It only took two months for Millie to conceive, and the pregnancy gave them something to dream about together again. They were both happy when Lucy was born, thinking this might give them a fresh start. However, managing life with two children was more overwhelming than they had anticipated. Millie became almost militant in her routine with their new baby and toddler as she tried to re-establish order in the house. Ethan and Lucy were on such a tight schedule and seemed to be thriving. Millie wore the "mommy" badge proudly and looked like she had it all handled. Those kids were her whole world. And shouldn't they be?

It didn't take long for Matt to again feel alienated from his family. He suppressed the jealousy he felt over the affection she gave to the kids yet withheld from him. Millie mentioned that she needed more connection and more engagement from him, but Matt had nothing left to give. His second job was starting to wear on him, and all he wanted to do at the end of the day was to eat dinner, unwind, and go to bed. Wasn't he entitled to at least that much? Matt was providing the home and lifestyle Millie wanted, and she had everything else under control.

Meanwhile, Millie grew more distant, barricaded behind her pain and rejection. She had put her heart out there several times. Still, she was baffled that Matt didn't engage more with her and the kids. Sure, he worked hard for them, but Millie became more and more convinced that the job was all that satisfied Matt. At least she had the kids. They moved through days, weeks, months, years.

They had settled into a comfortable rhythm, and Matt felt he was giving his wife what she needed. They lived in the house they had wanted in a great school district, just a block from some of their closest friends. They had become leaders in their church, Millie was a volunteer at their daughter's pre-school, and Matt coached their son's little league team. Their family pictures posted online had hundreds of "likes" and comments. They were the envy of all their friends. Days of busy turned into weeks of silence. Months passed with only logistical conversations for how to get the kids to and from their activities.

Their conflicts had ceased months ago, but so had any sort of communication. Recent evenings found Matt in the basement for hours, gaming or trolling the internet to defrag from the day. He had convinced himself that the pornography he had looked at a few times wasn't wrong. He needed to feel something. And after a long day filled with school and after-school events, cooking dinner, then packing lunches for the next day, Millie found herself falling asleep every night to the background noise of her latest binge-watch, alone. The days were cold. The nights were frigid. They both realized they were living together as strangers.

This adventurous trip was a last-ditch effort to help realign their family. However, as they sat side by side, with two kids in the backseat, Millie's words echoed in Matt's head as it was starting to sink in that she wasn't talking about the flat tire on the car. She was talking about the wreck their marriage had become. This trip, like their relationship was going nowhere. Not entirely sure of what would come next, Matt was finally able to respond with, "This is not exactly the adventure I signed up for either."

The Marriage Adventure

As Matt and Mille relayed the details of their trip in our first counseling session together, their words were all too familiar. I hear this story almost weekly as I sit in my office counseling couples in crisis. Based on the most recent statistics on failing marriages, you probably have a Matt and Millie living next door to you. If you're reading this book, there's a strong chance that you and your spouse can identify with them. There is no shortage of literature on relational issues between a husband and wife, so why another book on marriage?

Marriage is an adventure worth experiencing. Therefore, it warrants preparation for the journey ahead or remapping a better route when we get sidetracked. When we set out on a cross-country road trip, it's easy to become discouraged when we hit roadblocks or run out of gas in the middle of a deserted highway. It can almost be enough to end our adventure altogether. What if we could pull back from our singular focused windshield view and see God's overhead perspective of this marriage journey we are on? After all, He designed marriage and has the perfect road map if we are willing to follow it. Anyway, you slice it, marriage is an adventure.

The difference between a nomadic journey and a grand adventure lies in knowing where you want to go and how to get there. As we read scripture, it is evident that God is purposeful. In Isaiah 14:24, we hear the Lord of Hosts saying, "As I have planned, so shall it be, and as I have purposed, so shall it stand." God put your marriage and family together with a purpose and a plan. If we can envision the beautiful sunsets and oceans in the distance, we might find the courage to move through the desert places that take us there. That's the difference between a fantastic adventure, and one you regret taking.

Although I wish they would, I've never had a married couple schedule an appointment to tell me what a great relationship they have. Instead, they walk into my office in crisis. These couples are broken, hurting, angry, frustrated, and often desperate for a way to repair the mess they find themselves in. Or they are searching for biblical permission to get out of the relationship altogether. We have seen acquaintances, church members, and even close friends experience this slow fade of relational distress. Only a select few have come through it stronger.

We have the privilege of leading the premarital workshops at our church for engaged couples. They arrive with a twinkle in their eyes, full of dreams of the great adventure they are embarking on together.

That's why we love leading it. However, our hearts break to see some of those same couples return for counseling within a few short years feeling hurt, disappointment, and heartache from the pain they've inflicted upon each other.

The heartbreaking reality is that, according to the most recent statistics on divorce in the United States, although the divorce rate has dropped slightly from fifty to forty-five percent over the last two decades, it's not an indication that marriages are getting stronger.[1] On the contrary, the trend shows that fewer couples are entering into a committed marriage out of fear of it ending or because of their decreasing faith in the institution of marriage itself. If this is the case, then what's the point? With such a bleak outlook on marital bliss, is there a way to restore health to the relationships that God has intended to be the bedrock of a thriving society? Our hearts beat with the hope that couples can experience marriage as the incredible adventure God has designed it to be!

Matt and Millie showed up in my office that day, ready to take the first and most crucial step in repairing their relationship. They were both open and willing to become active participants in putting their marriage back together. It didn't happen overnight, but that day, they began to find renewed vision and purpose for their marriage. Together, they began to repair the flat tires in their relationship and move onward to their destination. So, what is needed to take an average adventure and turn it into the trip of a lifetime?

As we set out together on this exploration to define God's purpose for your marriage, we have no desire to give you a three-step plan to make you happier in your relationship. We believe it's much bigger than that! God hasn't simply joined you and your spouse together to have children, work jobs, buy new houses, go to church, make some friends, be happy, then die. You were brought together to accomplish a mission! It's far greater than you might think.

CHAPTER 1:

THE GREAT ADVENTURE

"I think I can; I think I can, I think I can." As Bonnie recited the monotonous phrase from *The Little Engine That Could*, I prayed, "Dear Lord, please get us up this mountain."

No, this isn't another story about Bell Rock in Sedona. This little incident happened several years ago as I was towing our little camper up the side of a mountain. The problem was I was pulling said camper behind a 20-year-old SUV that preferred a casual drive through the countryside, as opposed to a strenuous mountain climb. As I looked down, the temperature gauge on my dashboard was steadily climbing! I kept imagining smoke billowing from under the hood while a tow truck came to our rescue on the side of a mountain.

As the needle reached the brightly lit "H" (which stands for hot), we reached the top of the mountain. Whew. That was a close one. After this incident, we decided that if we were going to be an adventurous family, we needed a vehicle to take us to the action.

You need to understand a little backstory before I move on. Earlier in our marriage, Bonnie and I traveled on the road as full-time musicians in a motorhome. We LOVED that motorhome. We had so many fun adventures touring the country in that little RV.

Often, we would live in it for two to three months at a time. Basically, we were "van life" before it was cool. When we sold it, Bonnie was walking around the back of it and gently patted the bumper. I looked at the elderly gentleman who was buying it and said, "We might be a little emotionally attached to this motorhome." He said, "Yeah, you don't see a lot of bumpers getting love pats."

When we started looking for our new "adventure vehicle," we knew what we wanted and what we could afford. I scoured the internet for weeks. Just when I had convinced myself that this search would take a while, I found what seemed to be the perfect motorhome! It was the ideal size and interior layout. Even the price was right. Years ago, financial guru Dave Ramsey significantly "disrupted" our spending habits. So, we knew we'd have to buy an older model, twenty-two years old, to be exact, and renovate it. It was even older than my SUV. This RV was old enough to have gone to college and started a career.

The motorhome was located in Alabama, about four hours away from our home in Georgia. I told Bonnie, "These things don't last long on the market. I need to go look at it tomorrow."

As it turned out, Bonnie had a prior engagement and couldn't go with me to look at the RV. This is where we had to rely on our twenty-two years of marital trust. I asked her if she was okay with me going without her. With great hesitation in her voice, she said, "Yes." Honestly, it sounded more like a question coming out of her mouth than an answer.

We withdrew the cash (thanks to Dave Ramsey), and the next morning I set out westward to Alabama with a good friend of mine. When I first saw it, to be honest, it wasn't pretty. As I stepped inside, it only got worse. I caught a whiff of a horrible smell and actually thought that the owner's grandma had died in it! Basically, it looked and smelled like the 1990s threw up in it. But I had a vision in my mind of what this could be... so I bought it.

Four hours later, when I pulled up in our driveway, Colby, our 7-year-old at the time, stepped inside and said, "Why would anyone get rid of this amazing thing?" However, the look on Bonnie's and Josie's faces said something altogether different!

Bonnie reluctantly said, "I trust your vision. But you're going to need to get rid of that smell before I can help you renovate it." That evening, I started pulling up the carpet and vacuuming behind the cabinets. Suddenly, I found the odor. As I pulled my shop-vac nozzle out from behind the kitchen cabinet, along with it came a little crispy critter. All in all, I ended up pulling twelve dead mice out of the heating ducts!

Over the next six weeks, we pulled the carpet out, put down flooring, painted, and basically did an entire renovation of the inside of our adventure mobile. It looks completely different. It's our little home on wheels. Was all that hard work worth it? Absolutely! This past year and a half, our family has had so much fun going on adventures close to home, in what some friends affectionately refer to as "The Hoover Mover!"

Every time we return from a little weekend getaway, there's something in me that feels a bit let down. When the trip is over, I start longing for another one. There's just something in me that craves "next." Aren't we all a bit like that? Maybe deep down we all know we are called to a great adventure.

A Call to Mission

An adventure is a bold, usually risky undertaking or a hazardous action of uncertain outcome. Not everyone is daring enough to pursue such a great challenge.

Adventure implies daring to exert great effort and face inherent risk. It typically calls us to do something that not everyone can do. So, what allure does adventure hold for our hungry hearts? Deep down, we crave more than monotony; exhilaration over the ordinary, breathtaking landscapes along the roads we travel Intuitively, we know God created us for the extraordinary, and a quest for adventure holds the promise of the most scenic heights. But we rarely desire to travel this road alone.

There are few exploits in life more challenging or more rewarding than the marriage adventure. Sometimes we strike out on this journey with little certainty other than our choice of travel companion. Other times we've mapped out a route to all of the attractions we want to explore; a plan for occupations, homes, and children. We prepare for the big stops, but rarely anticipate the detours- unexpected job loss, illness, infertility, infidelity, or death.

Why do we feel this desire for adventure? Where does it come from? Why do we get bored seven years into our marriage when the journey isn't what we had in mind? Maybe it's because it is part of our design.

In the beginning, God created the heavens and the earth, day and night, the sun and the moon, land and water. Next, He made fish for the sea, birds for the sky, plants and animals for the land, and saw that it was good. If all of that wasn't cool enough, God crowned His creation.

> So God created mankind in his own image, in the image of God he created them; male and female he created them. God blessed them and said to them, "Be fruitful and increase in number; fill the earth and subdue it. Rule over the fish in the sea and the birds in the sky and over every living creature that moves on the

ground…" God saw all that he had made, and it was *very* good (Genesis 1:27-28, 31a, NIV).

Let's look at it like this. God crafted man and woman separately and uniquely and brought them together in the first wedding ceremony. Then, as they stood hand in hand looking out over this brand-new perfect Earth, the God of all creation gave them a gigantic, exciting mission. He put them in charge of filling the earth. He commissioned them with something so huge, so adventurous, that they needed to combine their strengths and work together to accomplish it. They were designed by God on purpose, with a purpose. His plan for your marriage is no less grand!

You may say, "But didn't God create Adam and Eve in a perfect, sinless environment? We live in the 21st Century. Life and circumstances aren't the same." Yes, God did create marriage in a sinless environment. However, He is omniscient or all-knowing. He doesn't exist in time as we do. Our brilliant Designer knew that Adam and Eve would introduce the world to sin. Even though God foresaw what the world would look like today, He didn't re-write His design or mission for marriage after the fall. He devised the plan for how the marriage union should operate, even in a sinful world.

Your marriage today can look like the original God-ordained relationship for husbands and wives. You have the ability to not only survive your modern-day circumstances, but to have a marriage that matters. He brought you together with a plan in mind and He has called you to a unique, grand mission, a great Marriage Adventure!

Marriage without a Mission

Twenty years ago, Bonnie and I were traveling to lead worship for an event in Kosciusko, Mississippi. (Can you guess what famous person was born in Kosciusko? Google it). Kosciusko isn't what you would call a large bustling city. We were travelling country roads for what seemed like hours. As we were driving along in our motorhome, we realized that I had missed a turn. Keep in mind, these were the days before GPS. If you've never driven a large motorhome, I need to fill you in on an important fact. It isn't easy to find a parking lot large enough for turning around a 24-foot-long vehicle pulling a ten-foot trailer.

We drove and drove for fifteen minutes or more in the wrong direction, just trying to find a place to turn around. The further we drove, the more concerned I became that we were going to be late for the event. Finally, I gave up. I saw a long driveway with a large pasture in the front yard, so I decided to go for it. I pulled in the driveway and attempted to make a U-Turn in the yard. I know I shouldn't have, but we would be late if I didn't do something! There was one problem. I didn't realize that it had been raining for the past three days.

When I drove on the grass, the RV sank like a ton of bricks into the muddy yard. We were stuck! My wheels turned and turned, slinging mud everywhere. Needless to say, I was horrified. I sheepishly walked to the front door ready to apologize. I was prepared to face the barrel end of a 12-gauge shotgun as I rang the doorbell. But the poor little woman inside wouldn't come to the door. Instead, she peeked out the curtains, probably scared half to death! To remedy the situation, I called the pastor of the church. He, along with some church members, pulled us out with a tractor. Again, I was horrified.

Most of us feel like we have a decent idea of where we'd like to be when our time on earth is over. I've heard many people say, "I just want to finish well." I agree. So do I, but that's not enough. Proverbs 29:18 says, "Where there is no vision, the people perish: but he that keepeth the law, happy is he" (KJV). This passage was a warning to the people of Israel to seek God's vision. Let's look at this passage again in the Message translation. It says, "If people can't see what God is doing, they stumble all over themselves; But when they attend to what he reveals, they are most blessed" (The Message). Let me explain it for you; if you can't see what God's doing, you will miss your turn and get stuck in the mud! Maybe we miss what He's doing because we aren't paying attention, or perhaps we're paying attention to the wrong things.

Like our money, time will budget itself if we don't set a budget for it. Time will get spent. When there's no mission, vision, or direction set forth for your marriage and family, the years will waste away. You may get married and buy a house, or two, or six. You may move your way up a corporate ladder, affording your fancy cars and big vacations. Perhaps you become a leader in your church, community, state, or even your country. You might have children and be their cheerleaders through school and a thousand extracurricular activities, then marry them off, so they eventually give you grandchildren. You spend your life saying "yes" to "next," running from one thing to another until you earn the right and the age that's ripe enough to retire. But what will be your legacy?

In marriage, when we don't seek God's desire for our future, we will miss our turn. We will senselessly wander down dirt roads. There are times it's an enjoyable drive on our way to nowhere, but hopefully, we'll sense that something is wrong and look for a turnaround.

When we seek God and ask Him to reveal His mission to us for our marriage, He will give a clear roadmap. However, like GPS, you may not see the entirety of the vision. God may tell you where to turn when you get there. What if we miss a turn? If you're a person that is seeking the Lord daily, He'll reroute you back on track. We'll talk more about that later in the book.

God has created us with a desire for purpose. We want to believe what we are doing with our days, weeks, months, and years will count for something. One of the most remarkable ways we can fulfill that is through our partnership with our spouse. Our marriage needs a mission!

Men Need a Mission

Men, take a walk with me (Daniel), if you will, back to a cool morning in a perfect garden. In the genesis of everything, we see that God created the heavens and earth, then all kinds of living creatures on land and sea. He saw that all of it was good, but then God did something really, really interesting. Before He ever created woman, He gave men our first mission. I have seen in the lives of men I work with and my own that men need a mission. Fellas, we were created to live on mission.

"Then the LORD God took the man and placed him in the Garden of Eden to cultivate and keep it" (Genesis 2:15, NASB). I love that word, cultivate. It literally means "to acquire or develop." Men, God designed us to be developers, creators, cultivators. He didn't design us to be consumers. He didn't create us to be lazy or apathetic. God gave Adam the jobs of tending the garden, which ultimately provided food to eat and guarding and keeping it, which speaks to active protection. As men, we should be hard-working providers for and the protectors of our families.

I have found that, as men, when we aren't living on mission, and when we're not focused, we get ourselves into trouble. Maybe you've heard the old saying, "Idle hands are the devil's playground." No truer words have been spoken. All sorts of temptations seem to find us when we get bored, idle, and unproductive, rather than keeping our focus on a healthy, God-given mission. In his book, *Play the Man*, Mark Batterson says, "You don't not sin by not sinning. You need a vision that is bigger and better than sin. You need a mission that demands every second of your time, every ounce of your talent, and every penny of your treasure. Then you won't waste it on lesser things."[1]

The majority of the men that seek out counsel for their marriage have fallen into one of two traps. Either they are putting so much time and energy into work that their wives feel neglected, or they have become so passive at home that their wives feel like they are living with a twelve-year-old boy, rather than a partner. Let's investigate this theory a little more closely.

When men dive into work, they get the sense that they are living on mission because they are passionate about their work. Or even if they aren't, at least they are driven to climb the ladder and make more money. They feel good that they are, in a sense, cultivating, and they are. Being responsible, working hard, and providing income for your family is a healthy God-given mission. However, we shouldn't confuse our sense of accomplishment with the fulfillment of our mission. Work should not be our primary mission. When our desire and passion for our jobs overshadow and exceed the leading of our families, we are sinning.

The year of my fortieth birthday, I went into a deep pit. I've had ups and downs in my life before, but never like this. For about six months, I was grumpy and crabby. I was a miserable person to be with. I probably yelled more in those six months than I have in my entire life. I have gone over and over it in my mind. Bonnie and I have investigated it, turned it upside down and right side up. Why? What caused me to go into this dark place? That was not me! I was pushing Bonnie away, and she was simply trying to keep the kids from irritating me. Though she didn't voice it at the time, she had even questioned whether or not I was having an affair. Believe me, I was not.

At that time, I was the Worship Pastor at our church and had just come through a season with the worship ministry that required great vision and change. On a larger scale, after walking through some difficulties, the church as a whole was healing and in a necessary holding pattern, which also included a spending freeze. With my pioneering tendencies, I perceived it as stagnancy.

On the home front, our children were young, and Bonnie was trying to balance everything there, along with her fifteen hours of work with me in our worship ministry. Instead of engaging with her, I became passive. She continually expressed her desire for more from me, but I continued to pull away. So, she had to take the lead at home. With her in a position of leadership that she wasn't designed for, I sunk deeper. I grew resentful of her, of my work, of everything.

I have always been a goal setter. Whether it was in ministry, personal, or family, I like to achieve. If you are familiar with the Enneagram Personality Assessment, I am the "Achiever Type Three." In this assessment, an Achiever is success-oriented, pragmatic, adaptable, excelling, driven, and image-conscious. I wasn't able to connect the dots when I was going through it, but looking back, I realize that this was the first time I had no apparent mission. Of course, I had a God-given mission, but I wasn't living it. We have now realized that was, in part, why I went into the "pit."

Many times, men aggressively pursue their jobs, their hobbies, or even their children's activities; then they come home exhausted and slip into passivity, essentially leaving the task of cultivating the home and family to their wife. He watches television, YouTube videos, plays video games, looks at porn, or in some other way, disconnects from the family. After all, he's taking a break from his mission of work, so he's off duty. A man has to rest, doesn't he?

This begs the question, "Can a man have hobbies outside of his family?" Yes. We all need things in our lives that rejuvenate and breathe life into us, and many times, our wife's interest will not be the same as ours. First, make sure that your hobbies are healthy and are not ones that will lead you into sin. Secondly, as you pursue them, make sure you are doing them in a way that not only breathes life into you but also breathes life into your family.

I like to run. From time to time, I get the itch to run a marathon. I'm not what I'd consider a "marathoner." However, because I'm goal-driven, every few years, I sign up for a race. I'm weird, I know.

Now, I can train for a race in such a way that makes my wife think, *Wow, Daniel is a much better person when he can get out, exercise, and have goals! I need for him to run.* Or I can train in such a way that causes Bonnie to get jealous and bitter because of all those stupid races I run! If it steals an excess of time, energy, money, and leadership from my family, Bonnie will get resentful. Then she'll have to try and provide some leadership in the void I've created. Feeling overwhelmed in a role she's not intended to play, she will attempt to control the circumstances and the person causing them, which would be me. Then her venting of frustration most likely comes across as nagging.

However, if I am careful to balance these areas and am not shirking my responsibility at home, she is not only okay with me having a hobby, she encourages it. Our pursuits should simply be a way to breathe life back into us to inspire us to continue pouring ourselves into the mission we're leading our family to accomplish.

As we have seen in the creation story, God hardwired into man the desire to be mission-minded. Guys, think of all our favorite man movies, *Braveheart*, *Rocky*, *Saving Private Ryan*, *The Shawshank Redemption*; all of these movies are about a man on a mission. There's no one more perfect to lead your family to be mission-minded than you! In the words of Rocky Balboa, "GO FOR IT!"

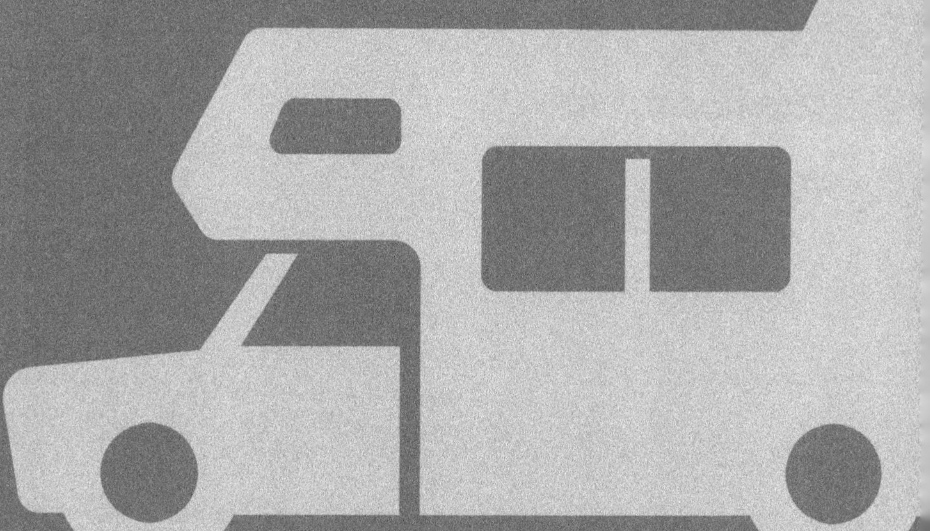

CHAPTER 2:

IT'S BIGGER THAN YOU THINK

Quarantine? When we bought the RV in 2019, we certainly didn't foresee a pandemic locking down our entire country just a year later. Our Hoover Mover spent most of its time sitting in our driveway. But we were thankful to have it when Bonnie suddenly became the online homeschool manager for Josie and Colby when their elementary school closed. I certainly didn't mind the short commute from the front door to the office on wheels parked in the front of our house during the quarantine! But as much as we've enjoyed using the motorhome for short trips and office space, I couldn't help thinking it was created for something bigger.

Since its initial makeover, we've ventured out on a few mini road trips. We have visited beautiful Lake Allatoona, a few miles from our house, surrounded by campgrounds; we love to sneak away to spend a few nights there. Dollar for dollar, nothing beats paddle boarding around a serene lake, then grilling up some brats (bratwursts, not kids) while listening to our favorite tunes. Though we love our little lake getaways, they still don't quite quench the thirst for adventure that made us dedicate six weeks of our life to renovating the best that late 90's recreational engineering had to offer.

There were many appeals to trading up from a pull-behind camper to a C-Class Motorhome. One was having the ability to be self-contained and run a generator when we are at our son's baseball tournaments for a day. In its first summer, it has already saved us some money in hotels for overnight games. Again, these tournaments are fun, but something was still lacking.

A few months after we bought the motorhome, I began to dream of taking a family road trip across the country. It's something I've always wanted to do but continued to say, "someday." As great as mini-vacations were, I longed to hit the open road and take an extended, unforgettable trip. One day I pulled up google maps to see how long it would take to drive from Dallas, Georgia, to the Grand Canyon. It would take eight days of roundtrip driving, 3,585 miles to get there and back. Okay, that's doable. If we're already out there, we might as well see Sedona. That added a bit.

Little by little, I added in stops. The Hoover Dam, then over a bit further to Los Angeles, up the coast to the Redwoods, Yellowstone, back down to the Rocky Mountains, and home past the Arch in St. Louis. All-in-all it looked like a 6,000-mile, five-week trip. I showed it to Bonnie, and she just stared at me with glassy eyes. After a few conversations, more mapping, and planning, we decided I would take a sabbatical and we would leave home after Memorial Day, 2020, to take the family summer trip of a lifetime!

Discovering Purpose

Do you ever get the feeling that your marriage could be more? Maybe you've accomplished a few big things together. You've paid off college debt, moved up from your starter house to your dream home, and added the number of children to your family that you desire. Maybe life has been good, even if it's not exactly been an adventure.

Our little motorhome has spent a few great nights in lakeside campgrounds and many baseball field parking lots, but it's never had the chance to take the long trip it was made for. Maybe you can identify with our Hoover Mover?

The only way to truly experience your greatest adventure is to live the life your Maker has designed you to live. What does that look like? The details are different for each person, and every marriage has a different path to adventure. But we will only discover it when we encounter a relationship with our Creator, who designed us with purpose. Think back to the Garden of Eden; God *spoke* everything else into existence, but *formed* us in the image of Himself. We are His image-bearers.

What does it mean for us to "be made in God's image?" In a 1971 article written by the founder of desiringgod.org, John Piper offered great insight into our design.

> We believe the image of God is not so much something that man has as something that man is. Humankind was created to be a graphic image of the Creator — a formal, visible, and understandable representation of who God is and what He's really like. The 'imago Dei' is not a quality possessed by man; it is a condition in which man lives, a condition of confrontation established and maintained by the Creator. The imago Dei is that in man which constitutes him as him-whom-God-loves.[1]

I love that wording, "him-whom-God-loves." Among many things, being an image-bearer means that God created us with a purpose; to have a love relationship with us. Unlike the animals in Genesis 1:24, we are not made "according to their kind." Humans were created in God's image. We were made to have a relationship with our Creator and resemble Him.

In his book, *What's Best Next*, Matt Perman states:

> My mistake was in not realizing that the purpose of my life had already been defined. You don't get to choose your purpose. It has already been defined for you, and it's the same for everyone. There are a thousand different ways we can say it, and we all need to state it in a way that is unique to ourselves, but the essence is the same for everyone.[2]

Rick Warren puts it perfectly:

> The search for the purpose of life has puzzled people for thousands of years. That's because we typically begin at the wrong starting point...ourselves. Contrary to what many popular books, movies, and seminars tell you, you won't discover your life's meaning by looking within yourself. You probably tried that already. You didn't create yourself, so there is no way you can tell yourself what you were created for.[3]

> God has stated the purpose of life throughout the Bible in dozens of different ways. The words God uses to describe it can differ, but the essence is always the same. The purpose of life is to know God, enjoy God, reflect His glory back to Him, and do this in community with others through Jesus Christ.[4]

Essentially, Jesus Himself is the purpose of life. He said this in John 14:6, "I am the way, the truth, and the life. No one comes to the Father except through me." Simply put, we find our purpose for life and for our marriage when we come into a relationship with Jesus Christ. But it's not something we can accomplish in our own power. God Himself pursues us and goes to incredible lengths to draw us into the greatest *adventure* we could ever imagine.

Adopted

Since we had spent most of our adult lives in ministry, we thought we had a pretty good grasp of God's love for us and the lengths He went to in sending Jesus to save us. But a detour on our marriage adventure opened our eyes to just how far God was willing to go to bring us into His family. We were married for eight years before we had any ideas of expanding our family of two. We had a great thing going and felt complete, until one day, God put a desire in our hearts to have children.

We'll share more details about this later, but we were naive in thinking we would become pregnant right away. Five long years later, we were blessed with our daughter, Josie, who is everything we prayed for and more!

Eighteen months after Josie joined us, we tenuously got back on the road of attempting to add a passenger to our journey. After six months and no sign of pregnancy, we decided to take a break, with plans to investigate adoption. We hadn't let anyone know we were trying to add to our family again, but God knew. Out of the blue, we got an email from someone that changed our lives. They wanted to see if we would be interested in adopting a baby boy that was due in twelve weeks. We instantly knew that this child was ours and reached out to the birth parents.

Over the next four months, we jumped through every legal, financial, physical, and emotional hoop that stood between our son and us. Though he didn't know us, we felt we knew him. While he was utterly helpless to reach for us, we pursued him. On the day Colby drew his first breath, we were there, hoping and praying he would be ours. He was legally born to his precious birth mom and given her last name. But the next day, we signed all the necessary documents to move him from her family to ours. They shredded Colby's original birth certificate and issued him a new one. This birth certificate forever seals him as a Hoover!

There is absolutely nothing we wouldn't have done to bring our precious boy into our family. And our Heavenly Father has gone to even more extraordinary lengths to bring us into a relationship with Him. The adoption transaction cost God His only Son. He paid with the blood of His son Jesus. Then issuing us a new "birth certificate," the Holy Spirit moved inside of us, sealing us in Christ.

> For those who are led by the Spirit of God are the children of God. The Spirit you received does not make you slaves, so that you live in fear again; rather, the Spirit you receive brought about your adoption to son-ship. And by him we cry, 'Abba, Father.' The Spirit himself testifies with our spirit that we are God's children. Now if we are children, then we are heirs- heirs of God and co-heirs with Christ, if indeed we share in his sufferings in order that we may also share in his glory (Romans 8:14-17).

We loved Colby before he was ours, from the moment we heard about him, and did everything possible to bring him into our family. In every way, Colby is our son. He has every benefit, blessing, and opportunity afforded to him that our daughter, Josie, has. There is nothing that can snatch him out of our hands. One day he will inherit half of all that is ours (basically a few dollars and several cool guitars!)

God adopted us into His family, which makes us joint-heirs with Christ! We gain a future home in heaven but already get to enjoy a relationship with God while we are still here on Earth. We get to walk in fellowship with God through a relationship with His Son, Jesus Christ.

Since Colby is in our family, he lives in our home, under our care and guidance. He abides with us, hangs out with us, fellowships with us, so he resembles us. He gets our jokes, has our accent, and enjoys our hobbies. Colby even looks like Bonnie and has her personality! Similarly, when we walk with God, we begin to look and act more like Him!

The Westminster Confession declares that, "The chief end of man is to glorify God and enjoy Him forever." We were created to walk and talk with Jesus, just as the first man and woman did in the Garden of Eden. As we delight ourselves in the Lord, the Bible says He will give us the desires of our heart (Psalm 37:4). This simply means that we hang out with Jesus and position ourselves close enough to hear Him when He speaks. The more time we spend becoming part of our new family, the more likely we are to understand the mission He is writing on our hearts for our lives and for our marriage.

Be Fruitful and Multiply

Though God created us individually to live in fellowship with Him, we see in Genesis that He brought the husband and wife together, then sent them out on an enormous mission. He joined man and woman, placing them in a literal paradise. They were there together when God announced their primary mission. "Be fruitful and multiply. Fill the earth and govern it. Reign over the fish in the sea, the birds in the sky, and all the animals that scurry along the ground" (Genesis 1:28, NIV).

In other words, God said, "I have a job for you. No! I have a great adventure for you, and you both have roles to play in it. You get to reproduce yourselves in the lives of others and rule over this kingdom I've given you! Go out together and conquer the world!" When God gave Adam and Eve the mission to "be fruitful and multiply," He asked them to make more image-bearers. He commanded them to make more people that He could have a relationship with.

Now don't miss this part; God called Adam and Eve to be fruitful and multiply BEFORE the fall. They still had alive spirits that were in perfect fellowship with Him. His desire was for them to fill the earth with more people just like themselves, people who could walk in a relationship with God, the Father. Then He gave them a kingdom to take care of and rule over together, and He saw everything He had made and decided, this isn't just good. It's VERY good.

Most of us get married because we have found someone we really like, share common interests with, and even love. We set a few goals: buy a house, have a few kids, save for retirement, stay married longer than our friends, but rarely do we set out on this marriage adventure, having determined our shared mission. Now, we know it sounds daunting when you consider the original mission given to humankind. Fill the earth with more people and rule it. Really? Currently, your only mission might be to get to the weekend without missing a soccer practice or forgetting to get a kid from school, or get through the evening without yelling at each other in front of the kids. Don't worry. We aren't judging you!

Adam and Eve had it good and messed things up when they ate of the one tree God said to stay away from. God warned Adam, "You may surely eat of every tree of the garden, but of the tree of the knowledge of good and evil you shall not eat, for in the day that you eat of it you shall surely die" (Gen. 2:16). Now, we know that after they disobeyed that they didn't physically die right away. Something far worse happened. The inner spirit that connected them with God died. They were left with a sinful nature from which they made all their future decisions- apart from God. The first humans lost their perfect connection with the Father and caused all of mankind to inherit their sin condition.

Fast forward a couple of thousand years, and Jesus came to Earth to restore our connection. He lived a perfect life and was crucified to pay for our sin. After His resurrection, He walked around on Earth, hanging out with His people. Jesus talked with them, ate with them, and told them what would happen next. Just before He left, He was very clear about what He wanted His followers to do. You might have come to know these words from Matthew 28:18-19 as The Great Commission:

> All authority in heaven and on earth has been given to me. Go therefore and make disciples of all nations, baptizing them in the name of the Father and of the Son and of the Holy Spirit, teaching them to observe all that I have

commanded you. And behold, I am with you always, to the end of the age.

Today, Jesus might have said it like this, "Hey everyone. I'm telling you this under the authority of God who made the heavens and the earth, the plan and mission have not changed. It's WAY bigger than just making it through eighty to ninety years of life without totally messing everything up. Listen up! Go reproduce yourselves in the lives of others. Go create more image-bearers, people that live in a relationship with God the Father! Go make more Christians! Fill this earth with people like yourselves and lead them to faith in Me. I am with you, and I'm giving you the power to do it!" In essence, Jesus restates God's original mission to Adam and Eve. If you and your spouse are followers of Jesus Christ, this is your primary mission as a family.

We believe one day when we're spending eternity in the new heaven and new Earth, enjoying a perfect relationship with God and all that He prepared for us there, we'll look back and say, "Why didn't I tell more people about Jesus? Why was I so concerned about my little world around me?"

God put you and your spouse together to walk in a relationship with Him. He wants His love to be poured into you both individually. Then as you mutually bless each other with the overflow of His love, that love overflows into your children. Next, it should spill out of your home to the rest of the world. Did you get the progression there? As you and your spouse individually walk with God, His love pours through you into each other, then to your children. But that's not all. This next point is the key. It should spill out into the rest of the world! As Christian couples, we are called to base our family's mission on the actual purpose of life.

Life on Mission

God has a plan and purpose for your family, and it's not just about you. You may be thinking, *but we have to live life. The kids have activities, and we have jobs. Are we to quit all of that and go door to door sharing the gospel?* Please don't! At least don't come to my door. One time when our kids were babies, I put a sign on the doorbell that said, "I already know Jesus, and unless you want to meet Him face to face, please don't ring the doorbell. Baby sleeping."

If we aren't to quit our jobs and everything else in life, how can we lead our families to fulfill the great commission? Let me ask you; why did God put you in your neighborhood? Why are you working at your particular place of employment? Why is your child on that ball team? The answer might surprise you.

We are surrounded every day by people who need to hear about the saving work of Jesus Christ. They not only need to hear about His love, but they desperately need to experience His love through you and your family. That is why God has planted you where you are and endowed you with your interests, gifts, and resources. Your mission will look different from ours because the people in your circle need *your* influence, not ours.

The enemy wants to divert our attention ever so slightly to the neighborhood's amenities, or to the ladder of success, or our kid's ability to get a scholarship one day. If we focus on those things, and accumulate more of them, then just maybe we won't even see the needs of the people sitting beside us or living around us. We'll be so consumed by the things *of* this world that we won't see the most significant needs of the people *in* our world.

Can we do both? Can we experience the simple pleasures of life and still be the light God has called us to be? Absolutely! However, the primary reason you do it is to live out the mission God has given every believer, to be fruitful, and multiply the life that He has put inside of you as Jesus shines through you. As we live our lives, we have to take our eyes off our own world and keep our eyes open to the needs of our fellow travelers. 1 Thessalonians 2:8 says, "Because we loved you so much, we were delighted to share with you not only the gospel of God but our lives as well" (NIV).

Intentionality with relationships is something that the two of us have repeatedly tried to instill in our little world changers. At eleven years of age, Josie challenges us to keep our eyes open to people around us who don't know Jesus. She has a tremendous heart for sharing truth with her friends, inviting them to church, and giving them Bibles or Christian CDs. She weeps for those she knows are far from God. We prayed two big prayers for that girl from the time we found out she was in the womb; that she would love God with all her heart and love people the way Jesus does. She understands her mission.

Our family has seen that living with a vision and purpose doesn't just work in theory. We have had front-row seats to how this plan can play out when we live on purpose. Our son, Colby, loves sports. Since he was two-years-old, he would watch nine innings of baseball and the entire four quarters of football games. When he turned seven at the beginning of the summer break, I asked him, "Colby, what is your summer goal?" He said, "Dad, I wanna hit a hundred balls off my batting tee into my net every day. I'm gonna hit fifty right-handed and fifty left-handed." That summer, he hit one hundred balls off his tee five out of seven days of the week and became a seven-year-old switch hitter!

However, Colby had one minor problem. He didn't play on a team! You see, we had established a family rule that stated, "you can't do an extracurricular activity until you turn eight years old." We made the rule because we love to camp and do fun family things and nowadays sports are all-encompassing. We didn't want to live at a ballpark when our kid was only five. We also sensed the window gradually closing that would allow us to dedicate so much time to just doing things together as a family, and we wanted to take advantage of what we had left of it.

Colby was so respectful of our family rule. We could tell he desperately wanted to play baseball on a team, but he never begged or challenged the rule. He was a sweet boy. Later that fall, Bonnie came to me and said, "I'd love for us to pray about letting Colby play a little earlier." Colby's birthday is July 4th, so if he waited until he was eight, he would have to play fall ball. Bonnie felt because of Colby's work ethic, his good attitude, and respect for our rule, maybe we should let him go ahead and play spring ball. After praying about it, we agreed that it was time.

That Christmas, a month and a half before the kick-off of spring ball, Bonnie and I surprised Colby with his very own batting helmet. Along with it was a note attached saying, "You're gonna need to wear this when you play spring baseball!" He cried. We cried. It was such a cool moment. He said, "I've waited my whole life for this!" And he had.

Let's fast forward a few months to April. Colby was loving playing on a team and all the attention he was getting for being a seven-year-old switch hitter! He was living his seven-year-old dream, and we were all having fun watching him.

Then, on April 8th, I got a text telling me that the father of one of the boys on Colby's team was killed in a tragic car accident. I gasped! Tears filled my eyes as I thought of this little boy without his daddy. Here's the kicker; he and his dad lived with his grandmother since his mom wasn't really in his life. As a pastor and a Christian, I knew I had to reach out. I called Suzy, the grandmother, and told her I was a pastor and asked if they needed help with the funeral. I let her know that I was available if they needed to talk to someone. Suzy and Levi didn't have a home church, so I spoke at the funeral and met with them for grief counseling.

From the time our children were very young, we repeatedly told them that life is about bigger things than just living it. In this case, baseball isn't about baseball. For us, baseball is about the people we play with and sit in the stands with and sharing God's love with them. The game of baseball is secondary. Sitting at the dinner table that evening, we told Josie and Colby about the accident. We reminded them that our job is to share the love of Jesus with Levi and his Ma-Maw. Remember, baseball isn't about baseball.

A few weeks later, Suzy and Levi started attending NorthStar (our church). Levi got plugged into our children's ministry, and Suzy started attending our Grief Share class. They have found a home and a community of believers that they never had before this tragic event. One night, Colby and I were lying in his bed chatting about Levi. I said, "Colby, do you know why God wanted you to play baseball early?"

He said, "Yes, sir. So I could be on Levi's team."

As we said our prayers that night, we thanked God for bringing Levi into our lives. A year and a half after God put Colby on that team, I had the privilege of baptizing Levi and Suzy. Even as we're writing this book, God is in the process of bringing a small revival to our current baseball team. God is drawing some amazing families to Himself that were previously unchurched and had taken a step back from Him. Six families are now attending our church. These are some of our favorite people in the world, and I want every one of them living on my street when we get to eternity! Baseball is not just about baseball!

Life isn't about what you think it is. One day, if Colby is a good enough baseball player to get a college scholarship or Josie is the valedictorian of her senior class, we will undoubtedly be proud. But if the children and families we have walked alongside through this life never feel or hear of the love of Christ, we haven't succeeded at accomplishing our mission. In the grand scheme of life, we would have missed our target.

When you and your spouse are walking in fellowship with Jesus and living with a common mission, it will affect the people in your life. As you live out Christ's mission, the world will look at your family and see a living and loving God. We all have a mission. The question is this, have you and your spouse defined yours?

CHAPTER 3:

MAPPING MISSION AND CORE VALUES

"I can't believe I let you talk me into this."
My head was spinning, looking at the highlighted route from our house to the Grand Canyon and back. Barely on board with Daniel's big idea to travel the country in a single summer, it was dawning on me how much planning it would require to pull off a trip of this magnitude.

You have to understand something about my personality. I'm not too fond of change and need time to warm up to anything that takes me out of my comfort zone. I needed to know every stop we would make on our trek, so I had time to prepare myself. I needed a road map defining where we were going and a detailed picture of the route we would take to get there. Daniel was patient with me as we sat down together over the next few weeks and mapped out our grand journey.

Have you ever seen how rice in a pot of water seems to swell and grow bigger and bigger? That's kind of what happened to this road trip. At first, it was just The Grand Canyon. While we're out there, why not make the best use of our time? So we added Sedona and the Hoover Dam. A few days later, Daniel said, "Hey Bonnie, The Hoover Dam is only a few hours from L.A. and the California coast!" It just kept growing over the next several weeks! Finally, we had to stop the insanity. The final plan was to drive to Sedona, the Grand Canyon, the Hoover Dam, San Francisco, Los Angeles, Hollywood, Laguna Beach, Big Basin State Park, Yosemite, Yellowstone National Park, the Rocky Mountain National Park, St. Louis, then back home.

With such a big trip ahead of us, we spent the next ten months planning and saving money. We said no to all the shorter camping trips that we would usually have taken. We visited family over fall break, skipped our yearly Christmas/New Year's trip, and gave up the short overnight lake trips that we had become accustomed to. But it didn't seem like a big deal, even to our children because we knew something bigger was coming. We had a mission... the summer *Hoover Super Trip*!

Unique Mission

I am blessed to serve on staff at a great church in the North Metro Atlanta area. At the time we're writing this book, I've been at NorthStar Church for 18 years. At NorthStar, "we exist to help people find their way home." That is our mission.

I'll never forget the day when Mike, our Senior Pastor, walked into a staff meeting and began to explain what it was like for him as a child when he would come home from baseball practice. He said, "When I came home, I always used the back door because that's where friends and family came in. I remember the sound of the old screen door closing behind me, and I remember the smell of that kitchen. I just knew I was home."

That was the feeling he wanted people to have when they visited NorthStar for the first time. We want it to feel like home. Not only do we want them to find a church home, but more importantly, a home in heaven. That day, Mike gave us a mental picture of what our mission was going to be. But we couldn't tell that story to everyone that walked in the doors, so we needed to develop a short phrase that was memorable and could be easily understood.

Over the next several weeks, a group of us met for strategy sessions to brainstorm and design our new mission statement. We also came up with five core values that represent things that are intrinsic to us as a church. Today, if you pull onto our campus, walk through our buildings, and talk to our volunteers, you would instantly know that we want you to feel at home.

Here's where it became difficult for me; after walking through his process for my church, I went home and looked around at the most important people in my life. And I realized something; I had no idea what our mission was. As the head of the family, I didn't have any guiding principles or a mission statement written down for why we existed. Do you see the irony here? We work 40+ hours a week for a company, and in my case, a church, and then we come home with no mission or vision for our marriage or family. God's mission and purpose for my family are way more important in my life than my job. There must be a bulls-eye, a target we are shooting for, to keep us moving in the right direction.

Isn't it enough to understand that God wants us to share Christ with the world? Why must we develop an actual statement? First Corinthians 9:24 says, "Do you not know that in a race all the runners run, but only one receives the prize? So run that you may obtain it." We have to keep our eye on the greater mission set ahead of us in our marriage. But that isn't easy to do if we haven't defined the prize.

Although Jesus gave all Christians the same common mission, it's expressed differently in each of our lives. Therefore, we need to understand how God wants us to live it out uniquely. The process of crafting a mission statement is just as important as the statement itself. When you write it down, you can memorize it, write or hang it on your walls; that way, you will see it regularly and be reminded to stay on your mission.

Every family is different. God has created each person and each couple with unique personalities, skills, likes, dislikes, and put them in various locations with varying amounts of resources. So, your mission statement will look completely different from any other family's. It's essential to spend time working this out together. Include your children in the process if they are old enough to participate.

A few years ago, Bonnie and I sat down with the kids and worked through creating a purpose statement and core values. It was a really cool experience. If you would like to do something similar, on the following pages, we walk you step by step and outline the process our family used, along with the finished product. If you feel like this process is too laborious for you, we encourage you to visit our website and use our online Mission Statement Generator. This online tool will walk you through these steps. This will help you focus and craft a mission statement for your marriage and family.

> Visit www.themarriageadventure.com/mission-generator. This tool will help walk you and your family through the process of creating a Marriage & Family Mission Statement.

One key point to remember: The process is just as important as the final statement you come up with! Before you start thinking about your family mission statement, decide together not to get hung up on whether it "sounds good" or "looks right." In reality, the end product isn't as important as the process – this task of creating your family mission statement is where the real magic happens. During the drafting process, you'll have a chance to have deep, meaningful conversations with your spouse and kiddos about what's truly important in life. You'll have the opportunity to bond and connect as a family and pray together as you empathetically listen to each other.

You and your spouse will be drawn together in a new way as you dream about the values and principles you hope will guide your family. Your confidence in your family will increase as you hear them share their ideas. Simply discussing values and principles as a family will direct your children to start thinking about God's purpose in their daily lives, which, in our opinion, is a big win in itself. What if you don't have children? Or your children are already grown? Is it still of value to have a mission statement for you and your spouse? Absolutely! When God gave Adam and Eve their mission, they didn't have children. If you are breathing, you need to know your calling in life.

As you work through the steps outlined below, don't get discouraged if you think it's taking too long or isn't going exactly how you wanted. In those moments, when you feel like giving up and retreating into default mode, focus on the process. Remember, the important thing is that you're intentionally starting a conversation and seeking God on what it means for your family to live a life on mission. This is a life-long, multi-generational discussion, so don't get discouraged if one family session doesn't lead to the perfect family mission statement.

The great author, Stephen Covey, inspired the following step-by-step guide. This is designed for a family with children. However, we believe it's a great idea for married couples without children or even empty nesters; simply adapt the steps to fit your situation.

Step #1: Pray, pray, pray

Pray as a couple, then as a family and ask God to begin to reveal to you HIS vision for your family. The more you fellowship with God, the more you will sense where He is leading you.

Step #2: Create a Memorable Experience

Think back on extraordinary, memorable events in your life. What makes them noteworthy? Most likely, you were having fun with people you cared about. If you want this process of making a family mission statement to stick, you need to make it fun!

Maybe you can take a family vacation and set aside a day to brainstorm a family mission statement. You don't even have to go far from home. Go camping, make s'mores, and sit around the campfire, or rent an Airbnb nearby, order pizza, and get everyone in their PJs. The key is to make the occasion different from any other "family meeting" or night of the week. You don't want it to come across as another family lecture.

Husbands, we suggest you step up to lead this meeting. While you will facilitate this process, everyone needs to have input; you simply serve as a guide to create an environment where everyone's ideas can be heard.

Remember to have a listening ear. If your kids start saying silly things, go with it. It's so rare that kids have input into household issues. They will love feeling like their contributions matter. You may discover that while you're on the same page on most things, you might be in completely different books on other issues.

You'll want to assign someone to be the note taker, to capture all the ideas that get spit out during your brainstorming session. It's a good idea to use a dry erase board or easel pad so everyone can see. Use colored markers or bright sticky notes. You could even cast a document on your television from your computer.

Keep it fun and engaging. The process is the most important thing. You don't have to crank out a completed family mission statement in one sitting! If it turns into a long, boring family meeting, your family will disengage. When you see them zoning out, feel free to stop and resume the next day. For elementary-age kids, keep each meeting under thirty minutes; if they're older than ten, forty-five-minute sessions are probably best. Just remember to make it age-appropriate.

Step #3: Brainstorm and Explore Big Ideas

Ask questions, read scripture, dream, and share ideas. Collaboration is the key to coming up with brilliant ideas. Take time to discuss what you believe your family is all about. This is a great opportunity to hear from your spouse and your children about what they think your family is like, as well as what they would like for it to become. By including every family member in the brainstorming process, you will gain a greater insight into their hearts and their view of your family unit.

The brainstorming process is meant to idea-share in a safe environment. Listen to every suggestion and voice, even from the youngest members of the family. Write down every idea someone shouts out, and remember that no idea is a bad one.

One of the easiest ways to open the floor for conversation is by asking questions. Here are some suggested questions from *The 7 Habits of Highly Effective Families*[1] to help you do that:

What is the purpose of our family?
What kind of family do we want to be?
What types of things do we want to do?
What kind of feeling do we want to have in our home?
What kind of home would you like to invite your friends to?
What embarrasses you about our family?
What makes you want to come home?
What do we want to be remembered by?
What kind of relationships do we want to have with one another?
How do we want to treat one another and speak to one another?
What things are truly important to us as a family?
What are the unique talents, gifts, and abilities of family members?
What are our responsibilities as family members?
What are the principles and guidelines we want our family to follow?
Who are our heroes? What is it about them that we like and would like to emulate?
What families inspire us, and why do we admire them?

How can we contribute to society as a family and become more service-oriented?

Question: Do the answers to the above questions reflect in any way The Great Commission Jesus gave us?

Step #4: Identify Core Values

Core values are the fundamental beliefs that you hold down to your very core. They are the set of principles, ideals, and beliefs that direct you in everyday life. A core value is something so central to you; you would risk punishment to hold to it.

> Core values are the handful of beliefs, guiding principles, or tenets that are absolutely non-negotiable within an organization. Imagine your own personal values: it may be that, in relationships, honesty, integrity, and kindness are important to you; you may value courage, fearlessness, and daring; or how about fun, humor, and happiness? When you contemplate your personal values, you usually have a sense of what is truly important to you- the characteristics you couldn't live without.[2]

First, make your list of values as big as you want – you'll condense it later. Here are some ideas to jog your thoughts: adventure, creativity, discipline, education, faith, fun, health, honesty, humor, God, integrity, kindness, service.

Next, brainstorm and compile a list of all the intrinsic, moral, family rules you have. These are the things you find yourself saying over and over. For example, "Love God and love people. It's never wrong to do what's right. How you do anything is how you do everything. Let your light shine. If it doesn't challenge you, it doesn't change you," etc.

Once you have this list, find similar or duplicated statements and cross them off. Then narrow it down to the 4-6 most important ones that really represent your core value system. These are a set of guiding principles that you will filter all of your activities through.

Step #5: Narrow Down

As with any brainstorm, you have to pare down that giant list of values and goals. The idea here is only to keep things that you want to include in your mission statement. This can be difficult because you don't want to "trash" someone's great idea. So, make sure to get everyone's input before pressing "delete." It's a good idea to narrow down to ten or fewer "big ideas" that encapsulate your family's mission.

Here are some ideas of how to do this:
- If some of the things you listed are just two words describing the same idea, combine them.
- Put a star by the values/phrases/goals/ideas everyone feels sure of.
- Then take the concepts you feel are important, but aren't sure if they're top 10 material, and put them in pairs.
- Think about two of those values side-by-side and ask your family which of the two is more important. Then eliminate the other. Keep pitting the survivors against each other until you're down to ten or less.

One idea is to give everyone a certain number of vetoes and votes to use. They can use multiple votes for an item they really like, but they can't spend more than their allotted amount.

Step #6: Draft Your Mission Statement

Now that you have all of your big ideas, it's time to pull them together into a single mission statement. It might be challenging to pull it all together, so be patient and do it in as many sittings as necessary. Here are a few things to keep in mind:

1. Keep it simple. This isn't for a fancy corporate plaque to hang in a business. You will want to put your mission into one or two clear sentences that even your youngest family members can recite.
2. Make it a team effort. Even if you come up with the final wording, make sure your entire family feels they have contributed. This takes more time and effort, but people tend to take ownership of their creations.

There is no one size fits all family mission statement. It will be as unique as your marriage and family. Therefore, your statement could end up taking any form you like. Some families write out their mission statement in one or two long sentences. Others list them in bullet points or print their values as a creative collage. This is yours.

Take as much time as you need. Write, edit, and re-write until everyone agrees you have defined your family's mission for life. The finished product is something you'll use as a standard and refer to for years and years, so it's okay if it takes several weeks to get it just right. Below are a couple sample mission statements.

Our family exists:

To love each other, To help each other, To believe in each other, To wisely use our time, talents, and resources to bless others, To worship together, Forever.

To encourage others to become like Christ through loving relationships, healthy lifestyles, and stimulating experiences.

Step #7: Make it a Work of Art

Now that you've created a mission statement and core values everyone agrees on write it on the walls! Not literally...unless you want to. Do something cool with it, and then hang it up in a prominent place in the house. You can let the kids have fun making it. Look for ideas on Pinterest, or put your woodworking skills to use. Create a plague or stencil it over a doorway. Then, you will have a constant visual reminder of what your family is all about and what you're working toward.

This idea of hanging your purpose in a place you can see comes straight from the Bible. In Deuteronomy, God gave His people commands to live by, a straight path of purpose to follow. Then He told them to display them!

Fix these words of mine in your hearts and minds; tie them as symbols on your hands and bind them on your foreheads. Teach them to your children, talking about them when you sit at home and when you walk along the road, when you lie down and when you get up. Write them on the doorframes of your houses and on your gate (Deuteronomy 11:18-20, NIV).

We want our mission statement to reflect our God-given calling and keep us on track! Bonnie had a friend build a really cool reclaimed wood wall hanging for our mission statement and core values. We hung it above our doorway and displayed the core values on our wall. We find ourselves referring to them often.

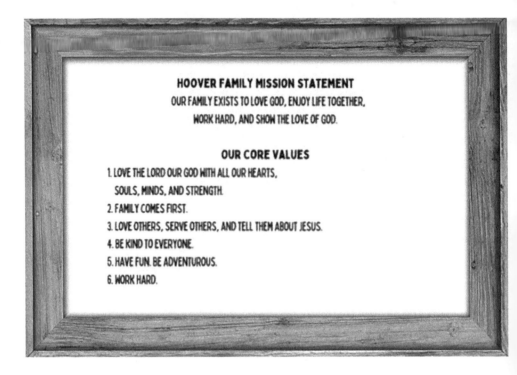

HOOVER FAMILY MISSION STATEMENT
OUR FAMILY EXISTS TO LOVE GOD, ENJOY LIFE TOGETHER, WORK HARD, AND SHOW THE LOVE OF GOD.

OUR CORE VALUES
1. LOVE THE LORD OUR GOD WITH ALL OUR HEARTS, SOULS, MINDS, AND STRENGTH.
2. FAMILY COMES FIRST.
3. LOVE OTHERS, SERVE OTHERS, AND TELL THEM ABOUT JESUS.
4. BE KIND TO EVERYONE.
5. HAVE FUN. BE ADVENTUROUS.
6. WORK HARD.

Step #8: Let Your Mission Be Your Compass

Like most home exercise equipment, your family mission statement is useless if you don't use it. Hold a competition to see who can memorize it the quickest, then let it drive everything your family does. Mapping your family's mission can create great teachable moments for kids. It can also help married couples make big decisions. This statement will serve as a compass as you navigate your marriage adventure!

The process of developing a mission may take quite a bit of time and prayer. Both you and your spouse need to have a voice in this process and share your thoughts and hearts about where you feel God is calling you to invest your lives. You may find that defining your family's purpose will draw your hearts together in a way you haven't experienced before. Dreaming together for your future can ignite passion in your marriage.

Having a clearly defined mission is one thing, but once you know where you are going, it's essential to begin plotting your course on how to get there.

Listen to The Marriage Adventure Podcast, Episode 15 to hear about the importance of having a family mission statement. www.themarriageadventure.com/podcasts

CHAPTER 4:

VISION

Four days. One way. That's how long it would take to get from our driveway to Sedona, Arizona, in the Hoover Mover. We are not sure how the children in your life face the prospect of being trapped together in an automobile for four days, but we knew we were going to have to make it sound good to ours. With the trip of a lifetime ahead of us, it was essential to get our then ten and eight-year-old children on board with us.

Besides a commitment to lots of driving hours, it would also take full family buy-in if we were going to sacrifice our usual trips and skim back on Christmas gifts to save for our summer adventure. At first, Josie and Colby weren't as excited about driving across the country as we were, but then we sat them down and pulled up YouTube.

For weeks our evenings consisted of watching travel vloggers and videos that other families had posted of their trips to the Grand Canyon, Sedona, the Rocky Mountains, and the rest of our intended destinations. Did Josie and Colby catch the vision? Absolutely! They were pumped! They even got a piggy bank labeled "Our Adventure Fund" and began dropping their spare change into it; all it took was a little vision.

Vision Casting

If there's one thing Bonnie and I have learned in our marriage, it's that I see the vision for projects, and she can put the details together to make it happen. With our RV renovation project, Bonnie could not see the finished project in her head. All she could smell were dead mice, and all she imagined was the hours of hard work it was going to take to get this thing in shape. Lucky for me, she had come to trust me and my vision.

Once we understand our mission, we must picture it to grasp what God has shown us fully. This process is called vision.

"Vision is a clear mental image of a preferable future imparted by God to His chosen servants to advance His Kingdom and is based on an accurate understanding of God, self, and circumstances."[1]

I've often heard the relationship of mission and vision put this way; mission is saying, "Hey kids, we're going to the Grand Canyon." However, if your kids have never seen the Grand Canyon, simply declaring that you're going there doesn't spark any excitement or passion. In walks vision. Vision is pulling up web pages and pictures of the Grand Canyon and watching travel vlogs of people who have been there. Now they are excited! They can literally see the mission.

Christian writer and researcher George Barna says that our mission is a broad description of who we are and what we hope to accomplish. Our mission statement identifies our most basic activity.[2] However, vision is specific, detailed, customized, distinctive, and unique. It allows you to say no to opportunities, provides direction, empowers people to service, and facilitates productivity.[3] Where mission shows us where we are going, vision shows us how to get there.

Once you and your spouse discover your mission and your mission statement, you will easily drift off course if you don't develop a vision for it. As discussed earlier, we know that God gave all Christians a common mission. That mission is to go to all the world and make disciples. This ultimate mission will be impossible unless we do two things; 1) cultivate a Godly marriage and family, 2) and direct our family's activities towards the great commission. Here is where vision comes into play. Developing a vision involves creating baby missions or goals. Goals are bite-sized missions. These goals will center around those two objectives.

How does a trip across the country help our family accomplish our mission? Bonnie and I had an objective for our *Super Trip*. Our goals were to have fun, build meaningful heart connections with our children, and create teachable moments and beautiful memories. Did we write these objectives down? No, but we discussed them as we dreamed together. That's one of the things that separates a marriage vision from an organizational vision; you get to have pillow talk and dream about wonderful adventures.

As you and your spouse consider new activities, projects, or things to get involved with, think of them as small goals that help you move toward your end-goal. Those will become your path, or vision, that moves you towards your God-given mission.

Aligning with Your Mission

Defining the mission in your marriage and family is only one part of the plan. The most challenging piece of the puzzle, especially for marriages that have been operating with minimal direction for quite some time, will be the process of moving toward health in this area. Once you have a new filter to run every family activity through, your next step is to align your family's time and resources to work toward that mission. This is an exercise that can lead to some family or couple disagreements, so it's vital to attack this issue as teammates.

Visit www.themarriageadventure.com/ aligning-mission to download a free pdf worksheet that will walk you through the process of aligning with your mission.

Steps for Aligning your Life with Your Mission

1. Set a time and place for the discussion.
2. Write down all the key components of your mission statement and core values (ex: work hard, have fun, be nice, etc.).
3. On a separate page, make a list of all the family's activities.
4. Make a chart. List one component or value at the top of each column on the chart. Make one extra column entitled "doesn't fit."
5. Place each activity in the column on the chart under the value or component it represents. This step will help you identify whether that activity fits within your family's mission.
6. If an activity doesn't fit under a column, write it under the "doesn't fit" column.
7. As you look at your columns, list the activities on another sheet of paper in order of importance. Do not add your "doesn't fit" items. (For example, church attendance or date night would be more important than a girls' night out or binge-watching Netflix).

8. Next, make a week or month in-view calendar. Begin to place the activities on the calendar from most important to least. You can add essentials like work and school if you'd like.
9. How does your calendar look? If the number of activities overwhelms you, then say no to the least important. If you feel like you need more, add some activities from the "doesn't fit" column or pray about how you can find more activities that fit your mission.

We want to give you a fair warning; implementation is where many couples throw their hands up and check out. This part is difficult because it may require sacrifice, and executing your vision won't happen overnight. You'll want to take small steps to phase some things out over time. It might mean downsizing your home to create a margin in your budget to help others. It could mean scaling back the extracurricular activities your children are involved in to make more time to enjoy each other as a family or to reconnect as a couple. In extreme cases, it might mean a job change or even relocation to move you in the direction God is calling.

We'll never forget when we were first trying to get our finances in order. We were only married a few years when we came across Dave Ramsey's book, *Financial Peace*. I was the spender/giver, and Bonnie was the saver/hoarder. Because we already made so little in the way of income, Bonnie could not understand why I would give away most of our paycheck and then turn around and want to buy a guitar. I mean, we were professional musicians, you can't have too many guitars! I didn't understand why she couldn't hear the voice of God when He told us to help that person in need. She kept saying, "But Daniel, *we* are those poor people in need!"

Learning to adjust our daily decisions under the mission of our financial goals was a long process. Back then, they didn't offer *Financial Peace* classes. All we had was the book. Since we were in the car a lot for our traveling ministry, we would take turns reading out loud as we drove. As I mentioned before, I'm a goal-driven person. Once we had a common mission, I was full steam ahead. However, having to say no to going out to eat on weekends wasn't comfortable. It challenged our resolve to save on more than one occasion. I look back and remember failing as many times as we succeeded. But after a few years, we had no debt, and we purchased our first (used) car with cash. We couldn't believe it.

That was only the first of many big financial goals we met together once we had a mission and vision for getting there. The discipline we learned during those early years served us well through the times we lived paycheck to paycheck while we were in our traveling ministry. It wasn't easy, but having a target on the wall kept us pressing onward during some difficult days.

When we allow God to write a mission and goals on our hearts, then persevere together to reach them, He will do far more incredible, and further-reaching things than our minds can even imagine. It won't be easy to accomplish our God-given mission. We can map out our mission, paint a clear vision for getting there, and still end up taking some unexpected detours.

CHAPTER 5:

OPPOSITION TO MISSION

"Well, I've got good news and bad news. Which do you want first?" I held my breath as Daniel walked in to give me the prognosis on his mechanic friend's inspection under the hood of the motorhome.

It only took a few weeks of concentrated effort to prepare for our *Super Trip*. Daniel and I put deposits down on all of our campgrounds and mapped out safe, free locations to stay on traveling nights in between destinations (that's called boondocking). I signed up for Good Sam's Club and put together a little travel notebook outlining fun stops along the way. Daniel also began preparing the motorhome to make the journey.

When we bought our twenty-year-old motorhome, we knew the inside would have to be gutted and put back together. Daniel was extremely excited about how well the outside had been kept up. It had been kept under a shelter for most of its life, so it had no leaks in it. And it only had 35,000 miles on the engine! We knew we could fix up the inside, and we counted on everything else to be in great working order.

Making weekend trips to a local lake is one thing, but Daniel knew a 6,000-mile trip would require the Hoover Mover to be in tip-top shape. One Saturday, a friend from our church who works on big engines came to our house to inspect everything under the hood and give us a run-down of anything that would need to be replaced. We had assumed it would need tires and weren't surprised when he said it would require new belts and brakes before we took it too far. But it felt like a gut punch when he pulled the dipstick from the transmission fluid and showed Daniel the metal flakes in it. Metal flakes sure are pretty, when it's called glitter, but not when it's on your transmission's dipstick. That's the downside to having low mileage on an old engine. After sitting for so long, the transmission deteriorated to the point it needed replacing.

"The bad news is we need a new transmission," Daniel explained to me as my heart sank. My husband, the eternal optimist who refuses to admit defeat, continued, "But the good news is we have plenty of time to fix it!"

The transmission was a disappointment. But we had a mission and were four months from leaving when we got it fixed in January before we were leaving in May, but that was only the first setback. You see, our big family trip was scheduled for the summer of 2020…the year of COVID-19. As you may remember, almost everything was closed down in June of 2020, even the great outdoors! Every major attraction and National Park we planned to visit was closed. With the entire country locked down to quarantine in March, we were forced to call the whole thing off.

To say we were disappointed is an understatement. It felt like all of our dreaming, saving, and planning was wasted. We took a few weekend trips to clear our heads during quarantine. We were hopeful that things would look better the following year, so we pushed as many reservations as we could to the summer of 2021. Now we have to wait another year.

Remember that longing for more? A few days before Thanksgiving of 2020, our gut punch was still lingering from six months earlier. That's when Daniel looked at me and said, "Bonnie, I feel like just jumping in the motorhome and driving out to Arizona!" The thirst for adventure was still raging.

After running through my mental checklist of all we would need to do in less than a month to get ready for this trip, I realized Daniel's idea was brilliant. Not knowing what 2021 would hold, he proposed that we take the weeks before and after Christmas and at least make part of our trip to see the Grand Canyon and Sedona. It wasn't what we had initially envisioned, but it was still a trip worth taking! A few days later, we had remapped our course, made new reservations, and were on track to leave three weeks later for an adjusted trip out west. No amount of opposition would keep us from completing our mission!

A Bitter Enemy

Mary and Allen were active volunteers at their church. We didn't know them well, but we were looking forward to getting to know them better after accepting their brunch invitation. We exchanged a few pleasantries, and when our breakfast arrived at the table, the reason for our meeting became more apparent. As Mary and Allen picked at the pancakes on their plates, we realized they were seeking our help to put their marriage back together.

Allen sat broken as Mary painfully described how she had become intimately involved with one of her male co-workers. At first, it was nothing more than a slight lift to her spirit when he would stick his head in her office and compliment her efforts on a joint project. Something in her whispered that it wasn't completely innocent, which is why she started bugging Allen to plan more date nights.

This is the part of the story where Allen put his head in his hands and wept. When he composed himself, he confessed that he felt partly responsible for what his wife had done. "I remember the conversations well. Mary was almost begging me for attention. But I brushed it off because my workload had increased, and I needed Saturdays to unwind completely. I wish I could get back the hours I spent rebuilding that old car and give them to her. I had no idea she needed more."

We returned to our car that morning, almost numb. Though this couple was desperate and both willing to put their marriage back together after the enemy had led one of them down the path of infidelity, we were ticked off. It was our moment of "that is enough!"

Have you ever had one of those? It's that moment when you are so hurt or angry at an injustice you've experienced or witnessed that your blood boils, and you want to scream at the top of your lungs, "THAT IS ENOUGH! I've had enough of this! I can't take it anymore! I have to do something about it!" Well, that's what we experienced that day. We were furious at the well-laid snare the enemy had used to lure another godly couple into, only to decimate their lives. The ember burned hot enough in both of our hearts to ignite a passion for propelling us to do something. Less than a year later, we launched *The Marriage Adventure* weekly podcast and blog.

Allen and Mary represent thousands upon thousands of couples who began their marriage adventure with a full tank of gas, an open road, and wild-eyed anticipation for the incredible journey ahead of them. They never imagined they would be ambushed and left for dead on the side of a dark highway long before they reached their destination. But that's the way marriages are most often torn apart when we least expect it.

If you and your spouse are walking in fellowship with Christ and working together to fulfill your God-given mission, you better believe that you have a target on your back! You have a very real enemy plotting to pull you off course. The devil had an agenda when he entered the Garden of Eden, and it has never changed. He is a thief who "comes only to steal and kill and destroy" (John 10:10). Satan's goal is the decimation of the body of Christ, and he intends to leave as much heartache and destruction in his wake as possible.

Why would Satan set his sights on marriages? One simple yet mysteriously complex answer becomes more apparent as we look at Ephesians 5:22-33. The Apostle Paul spends eleven verses talking about the husband-and-wife relationship. The most profound verse in the passage is probably tucked near the end and often quickly skipped over. "This mystery is profound, and I am saying that it refers to Christ and the church" (Eph. 5:32).

In His great love for us, God has given us the husband-wife relationship to serve as a beautiful illustration of the marriage between Jesus and His bride, the church. Through the finished work on the cross, Jesus has eternally united us to Himself. A grand celebration awaits us one day as we are forever married to our perfect Groom. The enemy is very aware of the reality of this pre-written happy ending for believers in the book of Revelation.

Immediately after Satan led Adam and Eve into temptation, God decreed an ending for the old serpent. In Genesis 3:15, He explained that as much as Satan attacks and wars with women, he will be defeated by her offspring. All the way back in the Garden of Eden, God had a plan to send Jesus to crush the head of our enemy. Satan can strike at our heels, causing us to stumble off mission and even walk with a limp, but in the end, God will make all things right again!

Although the fellowship between mankind and God was broken in the Garden of Eden, as God predicted, it has been restored forever through a relationship with Jesus Christ. This explains why Satan will do everything he can to attack your marriage. He won't ultimately win his war against God, but he sure can wreak havoc on God's creation. Your adversary wants nothing more than to keep you from experiencing a vibrant, Christ-filled marriage that points people to Jesus. It's no wonder there are so many potholes and so much wreckage along the road we travel on our marriage adventure.

The Enemy's Strategy

Though the reason for the enemy's attack is apparent, his strategy can be much more difficult to perceive. After leaving breakfast with Allen and Mary that day, we felt as if we had walked into the enemy's war room and seen the battle plan drawn out on the table. The devil cannot take out the whole Church, the beloved bride of Christ, with one massive nuclear attack. Instead, he plans to slowly erode the infrastructure by dismantling one marriage and family at a time. It's much like the homes we see dangling over the cliffs on the Pacific coast in California. Built for the oceanfront view, the homeowners never foresaw that decades of erosion from beneath the surface would eventually lead to their estate's collapse. It's a devious plan, brilliantly and effectively executed.

The enemy of all that God has ordained as "good" sneaks around, crouching in the grass, looking to pick off the weakest of the herd. That's why Peter warns us to: "Be sober-minded; be watchful. Your adversary the devil prowls around like a roaring lion, seeking someone to devour. Resist him" (1 Peter 5:8-9a). A lion hunts by carefully circling a herd, observing the weakest member, waiting to pounce when it is unaware and at its most vulnerable.

Make no mistake; Satan is circling your marriage, looking for a way to isolate you and deceive you. Maybe the lies are planted by way of voices in your head, speaking, *he doesn't notice me. I deserve better than this*, or *she doesn't appreciate anything I do, so maybe someone else will*. Or it might be the justification you are feeling, *it's fine to look at a little porn. I'm doing her a favor since she's not interested*. These are all lies the enemy sows. When we let ourselves dwell on them, the seeds take root and turn to attitudes. Eventually, our attitudes result in actions that damage our marital foundation and throw us off mission.

Little Foxes

One thing that sets marriage apart from any other organization that has a mission is the gift of intimate friendship between a husband and wife. It keeps us unified and moving in the same direction. Though we will devote more time to it later, it's important to help you recognize some of the enemy's traps that may lie in wait for you in the area of your intimacy.

If either of you is lured away by sexual or emotional ties to someone else, your entire mission is utterly wrecked. That's why it's so vital to guard it. One of the books of the *Bible* that gives us a glimpse into the depth of intimacy intended for marriage is *Song of Songs*. As the bride and groom euphorically revel in their admiration, desire, and passion for each other, the bride is aware of the possibility that something could spoil their relationship. She says, "Catch the foxes for us, the little foxes that spoil the vineyards, for our vineyards are in blossom" (Song of Songs 2:15).

> Listen to *The Marriage Adventure Podcast, Episode 36* where we discuss whether or not friendships of the opposite sex are healthy for our marriage. www.themarriageadventure.com/podcasts

An illustration about vineyards and foxes may not resound with us in modern times as much as it would when it was written. But any vinedresser would immediately link this to the threat the pesky creatures pose to the health of their vineyard and their livelihood. Little foxes are the worst because they can hide underneath the foliage. They sit and chew on the vine's stems and roots, going undetected, until they have done irreparable damage. We have to be aware of and diligently set out to catch the 'little foxes' that pose a threat to our marriages by putting boundaries in place to safeguard our most precious relationship.

The enemy most likely won't wave a flag to announce he is coming. He preys on our weaknesses, longings, unfulfilled expectations, and desires. He looks for a crack and often sneaks in unnoticed. We hope to raise your awareness of his tactic so you can search your own heart and fortify your marriage where needed. We have outlined a few things you can do and not do to catch the little foxes that might gnaw away at the roots of your marriage.

TO CATCH THE LITTLE FOXES:

DON'T
- *Don't stop pursuing each other.* Life gets busy, and we relax in our pursuit of our spouse. Be

intentional about spending time together. Choose each other over every other person (parents, friends, co-workers, boss, even children) and every other thing in the world (job, hobbies, phone). If we make this pursuit a priority, there are fewer opportunities for our eyes to get fixed on other people.

- *Don't assume you know each other's hearts.* As selfish humans, we don't tend to assume the best about other people. Satan will set your spouse up as your enemy if you aren't careful to know and understand their heart and motives. Because of this, you must communicate about all things, both big and small. Keep seeking to know your spouse's heart.

- *Don't keep your temptations and sins private.* No one is perfect. Everyone struggles with thoughts that are inappropriate or harmful to the relationship. But sometimes, those thoughts cross lines into sinful actions. That's why it's so important to talk about struggles and provide accountability for each other. Even be willing to ask your spouse the questions you don't want to know the answers to. Don't think you are protecting your spouse by hiding your indiscretions. The enemy does his best work in the hidden sins committed in the dark.

- *Don't let your guard down... EVER.* You must be proactive about filtering what you allow into your life and marriage. TV, movies, music, news sources, podcasts, social media, even friendships can all expose subtle entry points for a negative attitude and heart toward your spouse. It's also imperative that you set up clear and tangible boundaries about friendships and interactions with the opposite sex and often revisit them.

- *Don't wait to seek counseling if you need it.* One of the most effective lies the enemy uses is, "We're not that bad." Complacency and pride are roadblocks to health. The longer you allow issues to go unresolved, the greater risk you run that you become lukewarm, then cold and eventually bitter toward your spouse. Please don't wait until it's too late to seek an objective, godly voice to help you get back on track.

DO

- *Do learn to resolve conflict.* Conflict in marriage isn't bad. It's inevitable. One of the factors in long-term satisfaction for couples is their ability to confront issues in love and work together for a resolution. When things get heated and you begin to attack each other, instead of the problem, don't forsake the powerful words, "I'm sorry."
- *Do forgive each other readily.* When you live with each other, you will unintentionally and sometimes intentionally hurt each other. Forgiveness is one of the most powerful healing agents and protection from the enemy you can implement in your relationship. It's not easy, but it's crucial if you are going to be healthy and happy. Remember that the enemy wants to pit you against each other, so you mistakenly view your spouse, rather than your real adversary, as your enemy. This will cripple your effectiveness on your mission to build God's kingdom. It's a brilliant tactic.
- *Do enjoy each other.* It's not difficult to understand the concept that whatever you feed grows. Invest time in your friendship like you did when you began dating. Do fun things

together and have plenty of sex! The more positive experiences you have together will tip the scales favorably when you walk through the tough times in your marriage.

- *Do show each other lots of grace.* At some point, both of us are going to mess up. When our spouse blows it, our first reaction is usually to punish or hold it over his or her head for a later win. But when I am the offender, I desperately want my spouse to offer me grace. We kick the enemy in the teeth when we realize the undeserved grace God has shown us and extend it in that same measure to our spouse, even when they don't deserve it. At some point, we have to realize that our spouse is human and deserves a break. Marriage isn't about who is ahead or behind but about how we can show each other the love of Christ.
- *Do serve each other humbly.* When you serve your spouse, you follow the example Jesus gave His disciples in the upper room shortly before his crucifixion. Not only did He give Himself up through His death, but He also placed himself beneath them as He served them with His life. "Let each of you look not only to his own interests but also to the interests of others. Have this mind among yourselves, which is yours in Christ Jesus, who, though he was in the form of God, did not consider equality with God something to be grasped, but emptied himself by taking the form of a servant, being born in the likeness of men. And being found in human form, He humbled Himself by becoming obedient to the point of death, even death on a cross" (Phil. 2:5-8).

Protecting your marriage from the small things and working to cultivate the "vineyard" is tough! You have to put up impenetrable boundaries around your relationship and keep checking to make sure they don't have cracks in them. At the same time, you have to continue maintaining the relationship from the inside to ensure healthy growth. We know this sounds like a daunting task. That is why it's so important for both of you to be experiencing daily fellowship with Christ.

As much as you nurture the branches that produce grapes and protect them from pestilence, they won't yield healthy fruit if they are cut off from the vine or uprooted from the soil. There has to be a life source that delivers nutrients to the branches to produce grapes. That's why Jesus said, "I am the vine and you are the branches. Whoever abides in me will bear much fruit... apart from me you can do nothing" (John 15:5).

Nothing about what we are proposing is natural. The task ahead of you to work together to fulfill your mission, while maintaining an intimate friendship, is impossible in your strength, especially if you want your marriage adventure to go the distance over fifty to sixty years! God knows this. That's why He sent his Son, Jesus, to suspend His power as God, live as a man, and endure temptations and trials as we do. Jesus made His mission on earth to "do the will of him who sent me and to accomplish his work," (John 4:34) and "do nothing of his own accord, but only what he sees the Father doing. For whatever the Father does, that the Son does likewise" (John 5:9).

Jesus' mission was to give His perfect life to make it possible for imperfect people, like us, to have a way to live forever with God. Until Jesus, that was not humanly possible. But He accomplished it by staying in perfect fellowship with God. His relationship with the Father gave Him power and strength for living rightly. Through Jesus' resurrection from the dead, we have access to that same power to carry out the purpose of loving people well and leading them into a relationship with God.

Don't let your guard down for a moment in your relationship. There is, indeed, a very real foe who wants to rob you of all you hold sacred in life. The journey you are on with your spouse will take many dips and unexpected curves. Keep your eyes on the road and keep watch for the enemy's schemes. Your uniquely designed marriage adventure is worth fighting for!

CHAPTER 6:

TEAM LEADER

As you read in the opening lines of this book, climbing 4,500 feet up the side of Bell Rock in Sedona was not on my agenda for our perfectly planned adventure. I had researched enough to know that the ascent would be a bit much for us, especially with two kids in tow. We planned to follow the trail around the base of the mountain and maybe a little way up the easy part. With every trail marker we passed, I noticed the crowds dwindling. At one point, I wasn't even sure we were on a proper trail. However, we continued blindly following the handful of people ahead of us and kept going up.

At one point, we reached an area where we couldn't go any higher (without ropes.) I knew when my nine-year-old dare-devil was too frightened to move that we might have gone too far. See, Colby has no fear, and we were pleasantly surprised he survived visiting the Grand Canyon without falling in!

Colby was frozen in place, Josie was in tears, and it took everything in me to keep from breaking down. At that moment, Daniel looked at me and calmly said, "Are you alright?" In a whisper that the kids couldn't hear, I admitted, "No."

Daniel looked me in the eyes and in a firm voice said, "We're going to get down from here. I promise."

He then reached out his hand and guided me to a safer spot to rest. After he tried to find a safer exit strategy and couldn't, he went ahead of us and helped cautiously guide each one of us back down the mountain.

Team Structure

God has an incredible plan for every marriage. The scope of His universal plan is far too great for one person to accomplish, so He has given us a teammate to lighten our load on the journey. When husbands and wives know what they are called to and envision how to get there, it will take a tremendous amount of teamwork to reach their destination. One of the foundations of teamwork is for every player to understand the structure of the team and the role they play on it. Before we can work to accomplish our mission, we have to first understand our God-defined role in our marriage.

It would have been nice if we had understood the safety procedures of mountain climbing *before* we attempted to scale Bell Rock. Climbers typically climb in pairs using a safety system of ropes and harnesses. Each has specific tasks to perform as they work together to reach great heights and make it back down unscathed.

In marriage, as we work together to accomplish our mission, our talents, likes, and dislikes may dictate specific functions we serve in the relationship. However, those don't change the original order that God set up for the leadership of the family. Just like Mountain climbing has a specific order of operation, so does our marriage. Even if a husband turns the checkbook and yard work over to his wife because she is better at it, he MUST remember not to relinquish the God-assigned responsibility as the leader of his family. Every team requires a coach or leader and whether we like it or not, God has assigned one for the family.

We mentioned Ephesians 5:22-33 in the last chapter. It is a passage of scripture that you have most likely read or heard before. It tends to be controversial in the secular world and even in many churches. It's viewed as archaic even though it's read at many weddings. It's one of those verses that we don't truly feel like we can achieve and probably don't genuinely believe can happen. It sounds nice, but we take it with a grain of salt. However, if you want a healthy, godly, grace-filled marriage, it must reflect this passage. With that said, let's spend some time looking at it.

> Wives, submit to your own husbands, as to the Lord. For the husband is the head of the wife even as Christ is the head of the church, his body, and is himself its Savior. Now, as the church submits to Christ, so also wives should submit in everything to their husbands.

> Husbands, love your wives, as Christ loved the church and gave himself up for her, that he might sanctify her, having cleansed her by the washing of water with the word, so that he might present the church to himself in splendor, without spot or wrinkle or any such thing, that she might be holy and without blemish. In the same way husbands should love their wives as their own bodies. He who loves his wife loves himself. For no one ever hated his own flesh, but nourishes and cherishes it, just as Christ does the church, because we are members of his body.

> "Therefore, a man shall leave his father and mother and hold fast to his wife, and the

two shall become one flesh." This mystery is profound, and I am saying that it refers to Christ and the church. However, let each one of you love his wife as himself, and let the wife see that she respects her husband (Ephesians 4:22-23; 31-33).

Head of the Family

Now, we know what you're thinking, but please be patient and stay with us because this is good news. Paul opens this passage with a directive to wives, but within that, makes a statement about the leadership of the family. As a couple, we are to understand that there is an authority hierarchy or structure that has been given for the home. It is clear that the things Paul commands aren't determined by culture nor achieved by cultural methods. His statements about a husband's and wife's roles are based on the relationship between Christ and the church, which does not change.

Through the marriage relationship, God intends to paint a beautiful picture of Christ's relationship with His bride, the church. Just as Christ is the head of the church, Paul states that the husband is appointed head of his family. Yes, we said it. The husband is the head of the family. You might say, "I don't like that, or I don't believe that." Sorry to say this, but God didn't ask us if we liked it. He has a reason.

Pastor Jack Hibbs says, "If you have a good man who loves the Lord, every woman who does is happy that her man is the head, when marriage is done right."[1] That is the key. Pastor Jack goes on to say, "The word is given by an order. God has established a form of government that operates in the way of civics and theology. God has an order of ranking for government. It's true in government, business, the church, and God says it's true in the home."[2] He shared that Dr. Warren Wiersbe once wrote; "The man in the army who holds the rank of private could very well be a better man than he who is the general. But he is still private by rank. Position and authority may not be equal to character, but God has established his order."[3]

Responsibility

My experience at the top of Bell Rock was a bit different from Bonnie's. Looking over my shoulder, I saw a panoramic scene as I've only seen in movies or pictures. It's one thing to see God's creation from the ground. It's another thing to see it from 4,500 feet in the air. The majesty of the Red Rock formations against the skyline is simply breathtaking!

The old saying is true, "You have to climb the mountain to get the view." I was in heaven. With every step, every handgrip, I felt the adrenaline flowing through my veins. And then it happened. When I finally paused long enough to look into the faces of my wife and children, I didn't see the same passion and excitement. I saw fear.

My exhilaration turned to reality with thoughts of, *what have I done? Did I lead them to a place that isn't safe? Was this irresponsible? No one protested the climb!*

I was reminded of a valuable lesson that day. Often, as men, our passion and desire for adventure or for purpose, as pure as they may be, have to be kept in check by the ones we love the most. I almost let my desire to forge ahead create a disastrous scenario for my family.

To be the head of the family implies both accountability and responsibility. The head is responsible for what the body does. As Executive Pastor at my church, I am responsible for my team or staff and the things they do. You have probably heard the quote, "Everything rises and falls on leadership." The same is true for the home. The head is responsible and accountable for those under his charge. Husbands, we can't blame our wives for lack of spiritual direction in our homes, that's on us.

We discussed earlier that before God ever created Eve, He gave Adam the responsibility of tending the garden and protecting it. We also see in Genesis 2:8 that God commanded Adam, "You may surely eat of every tree of the garden, but of the tree of the knowledge of good and evil you shall not eat, for in the day that you eat of it you shall surely die." God gave Adam the responsibility for the spiritual direction of his family before Eve's existence.

It seems easy to lay blame for the first sin on the woman's shoulders. But if we examine the text closely, we see in Genesis 3:6 this little phrase that states, "she took of its fruit and ate, and she also gave some to her husband who was with her."

Whether Adam was silently standing next to her as she was tempted or if he was elsewhere and she brought the fruit to him, it is clear that Adam did not lead Eve away from sin, but also partook. God had given the command to Adam and it was his responsibility to impart the truth to his wife. He failed to lead her spiritually, and he failed to step up and protect her from the schemes of the serpent.

One of our all-time favorite movies is *Remember the Titans*. One coach sets out to integrate a football team in Alexandria, Virginia in the midst of volatile racial tensions in 1971. It wasn't going particularly well, as the team captain and another player couldn't move past their hatred for each other. In an intense argument, the captain asked the player about why he had a poor attitude on the field. The player looked at the captain and said, "Attitude reflects leadership, Captain." It was an incredible turning point in the movie as they both realized that the responsibility for forward movement rested on their shoulders as leaders. Once they began leading in the right direction, their teammates followed.

Men have been assigned the responsibility of spiritual leadership in the family, and nine times out of ten, wives willingly follow a loving, grace-filled husband who is serving and leading the family spiritually. Whether in the path of righteousness or destruction, or up the side of a steep rock in Sedona, AR!

Our culture is trying to rewrite what it means to be a man, and don't get me wrong, some things need to be rewritten, but we can't look to culture to define this for us. Guys, if you want a perfect example of a man that was tough, compassionate, a servant who relentlessly stayed on His mission without apology, look to Jesus. Our families need men who will step up and lovingly yet purposefully lead them—not squashing their voice but helping them use it. Men, I encourage you to "man up" and dig into this understanding of what it means to lead your family. If you need help, seek out a mentor or a local pastor.

Being head of your family is not easy. It's not a status that places you above your wife as your subordinate. Paul explains that you are positionally the head and carry the weight of responsibility, but then he elaborates on what kind of heart and attitude that requires. Ephesians 5:25 commands us, "Husbands, love your wives, as Christ loved the church and gave himself up for her." The husband's primary responsibility is to love his wife.

What does this type of love look like? Paul says, "as Christ loved the church." That's a tall order since Christ loved the church by serving and dying for the church. Husbands, we love our wives by washing dishes, keeping the house in good working order, changing a diaper, etc.; essentially, by being a man.

Love

Paul further says in Ephesians 5:29, "For no one ever hated his own flesh, but nourishes and cherishes it, just as Christ does the church." Words like "nourish" and "cherish" seem like words that women would be better at than men, but knowing it doesn't come naturally to us, scripture is clear that men are called to love, cherish, nurture, and serve their wives. That doesn't sound like dictatorial leadership, but a picture of servant leadership.

I've had men tell me that nourishing and cherishing doesn't come naturally to them. That is until I look at their pick-up truck or their fantasy football league. Men, we do know how to nourish and cherish things, sometimes just not the right things. What if we could show our wives and children the same love and devotion we do our hobbies, the cherished bass boat, or the man cave? Remember how you pursued your wife when you were dating? She needs to know you desire her as much today as you did then.

Loving your wife can be as simple as noticing she needs help with the children or housework and stepping up without being asked. It could be she needs to hear the words, "I love you," or "you look hot in that outfit." If she's a quality time kind of girl, dinner dates or initiating the occasional shopping trip together may make her feel loved. Sometimes loving your wife means you cuddle on the couch and watch a Hallmark movie without the expectation of sex. We know how to show love. But over time, we forget to make it a priority.

There's a little phrase that I have to remind my kids of frequently. I say, "Kids, what's our job?"

And they say in unison, "To make momma's life easier!"

Bonnie is the hardest working servant in our home. I can't out serve her, but I sure try. By trying to out-serve her, out-work her, and train our children to do the same, I am loving her. That's what Christ's love looks like! Do I always feel like doing this? Nope.

One of the worst feelings is when I'm in a hurry and I go to put a dish in the dishwasher and it's locked. You know what it means when the dishwasher is locked? It means that there are clean dishes in there that need to be unloaded. Whenever I discover a locked dishwasher, I go through this whole conversation in my head and heart. It goes like this; (tug, tug) …

Daniel: *Ugh. The dishwasher needs to be unloaded. Maybe if I just act like I didn't tug on it, I won't have to unload it.*

Holy Spirit: *"Really Daniel? She only cooks every night and keeps the house running. She doesn't have any more free time than you do. It takes three minutes. Unload the stupid dishwasher!"* (Yes, I timed it. It literally takes three minutes to unload the dishwasher.) Guess what I do; I unload it.

Then Bonnie says, "Awe, thank you for unloading the dishwasher." That makes her feel loved and secure. In reality, it's all because God smacked me upside the head, so I can't take credit for it.

Our families' leadership is to be taken seriously, as it reflects the leadership of Christ and His bride, the church. Christ loved His bride so much that He gave His life to pursue and bring her into relationship with Himself. He gave us the ultimate picture of what dying daily to ourselves in order to serve our spouse looks like. God wants to use us as a conduit of His love to our spouse. Husbands, the climate of your home is set by your leadership. "Attitude reflects leadership, Captain."

CHAPTER 7:

LIFESAVER BESIDE HIM

"Stop! That's close enough!" At every photo stop along the Grand Canyon's unfenced gorge, I could feel the stares from strangers as I barked my motherly orders at Colby. By evening, I felt like I had finished a strenuous abdominal workout, realizing I had been tensed up for hours, anticipating danger. There's nothing like being the killjoy on an adventurous family vacation!

Daniel reminded me time and time again that he wouldn't let any of us do something dangerous. I agreed to loosen up when he promised to pull back when I insisted. Knowing I am more cautious by nature, I have to lean into his adventurous side. We talked about it in private later, and Daniel also acknowledged his need for my ability to see potential danger. We struck a balance.

On day two at the Grand Canyon, I offered up my strengths of map reading, encouragement for our small weary female hiker, and occasional warnings for the small testosterone-driven one, but let Daniel take the lead. It was a much better day for everyone. I stayed in my lane, stuck to what I was good at, and learned to look away.

Helper?

Early in our marriage Daniel and I learned to work well together. We traveled to churches and student camps leading worship, teaching workshops for student worship teams, and we eventually began hosting conferences for church worship bands to attend. Daniel always had a dream for something big and I had the gift of figuring out how to accomplish it. We like to say that we work together like we paint a room; Daniel does all the big stroke roller work and I come back to do all the cut in work with the paintbrush.

We had a great rhythm to our teamwork in ministry. In 2006, when God called us to stop traveling and come on staff full time at our church, I sensed a potential threat to the dynamic of our partnership. For the first time in our marriage, we had co-workers who were incredibly good at their jobs. I spent several years struggling through my insecurities. With Daniel surrounded by people, even other females, who were much more gifted than I was in the roles I had filled in our ministry together in past years, I wrestled with fear and thoughts like, *will he still need me? Am I replaceable as his helper?* You see, as much as men need a mission, I believe that women need to be needed.

If we are going to accomplish our mission in marriage, it's vital to understand the unique roles we can play that will most benefit the team. When we are operating as a unit with a common mission, we are functioning the way God designed from the beginning. Man's need for a mission is part of his design and works into the roles he should play as cultivator, provider, and leader of his family. God has also written passions onto the hearts of His "Eves" that make them perfect teammates for his "Adams."

After God put Adam alone in a great big garden with a gigantic mission of protecting and cultivating it, He recognized the first thing in all of His creation that was NOT good. "Then the Lord God said, 'It is not good that the man should be alone; I will make him a helper fit for him'" (Gen. 2:18). God created man with a drive and need for a mission. However, the mission of man was far too big to be accomplished alone, so God created a helper that was suitable for him.

Now, I am a pretty confident woman, secure in my identity in Christ, but I have to admit to you that there's something inside me that wanted to tilt my head a little when I typed the word "helper." In fact, I looked up that verse in not two or three, but in SIX different translations. You know what? No matter what translation I read, I couldn't get the molecules to move around on the page to represent anything other than the word "helper."

Even though I grew up in a Bible-believing, church-attending, family, I will admit that I have allowed culture to slightly influence my view of the purpose of a woman in marriage. There's something within most of us that tends to minimize the role of a helper and view it somehow as a lesser role. Allow me to me assure you, the role of a woman, by God's design, is vital and irreplaceable. I love how Stasi Eldredge captures the essence of what it means to be a helper in her book, *Captivating*:

> When God creates Eve, he calls her an *ezer kenegdo*. Hebrew scholar Robert Alter, who has spent years translating the book of Genesis, says that this phrase is "notoriously difficult to translate. The various attempts we have in English are helper or companion or the notorious help meet." Alter is getting close when he translates it "sustainer beside him."

The word *ezer* is only used twenty other places in the entire Old Testament. And in every other instance, the person being described is God himself, when you need him to come through for you desperately (Deuteronomy 33:26, 29; Psalms 121:1-2; Psalm 20:1-2; Psalm 33:20, Psalm 115:9-11). Most of the contexts are life and death, by the way, and God is your only hope. Your *ezer.* If he is not there beside you... you are dead. A better translation therefore of *ezer* would be "lifesaver." *Kenegdo* means alongside, or opposite to, a counterpart.[1]

Okay! I can live with that! God had a mission too big for man to accomplish alone, so He created woman to come alongside him as his "lifesaver." She has completely different strengths than he does. She's wired to see things differently, catch the things he misses, strengthen his weaknesses, to make them an unstoppable team...when they work together and play the roles they were created to play. It's the same with the church. Each of us have unique gifts and abilities that work together to serve the larger body. The body cannot function properly without a head, arms, legs, eyes, mouth, etc.; every part is essential. God has given us unique gifts to serve within the body to make it healthy, just as He has created husbands and wives to work together in their relationship roles to fulfill their mission as a couple.

I understand how wildly unpopular this is in current culture, but I don't think it was accidental that scripture points out, "God created man in his own image, in the image of God he created him; *male* and *female* he created them" (Gen. 1:27). They were different from each other. They were uniquely male and female, yet they each bore the image of God. God had a purpose for designing us with different physical attributes and with specific roles to play in His plan.

The calling of a helper is not a small one, it is essential. When discussing the woman's role in marriage, Dorothy Patterson, D. Theol., explains, "helper is a precious wonderful term and God uses it to describe himself, and when he comes to help us, he doesn't divest himself of his deity. No, he brings all of that with him when he comes to give us aid and help us. And so a wife was created from the beginning to be a helper to her husband."[2]

All sixteen times we see God referred to as "helper," translated *ezer*, the passages speak with urgency and the need for God to rescue powerfully. Whether we are willing to admit it or not, I believe God has written on the heart of every married woman a desire to play an indispensable role in carrying out a grand mission with her husband.

My desire to be needed by Daniel wasn't the problem in my marriage those many years ago. The rub came in my attempt to MAKE Daniel need me. In my efforts to control his need for me, I was holding on too tightly. Instead of being a "lifesaver" and breathing life into Daniel, I was choking it out of him. So, what do we do with this longing to be part of something bigger than ourselves alongside our husbands? For starters, we don't set ourselves up to compete against or to control them. Instead, we have to ask the Lord to show us how we are uniquely gifted to work alongside our husbands in a way that only we can.

The problem is not in our desire to be irreplaceable to someone. Sin enters the equation when we allow that yearning to create codependency on others, whether it's our spouse, a friend, or our children. Although God designed us to live in community and in relationships, He has no intention for them to replace Him in our lives. No matter how devoted and wonderful our husbands may be, they make terrible idols. Likewise, our children cannot live up to the pressure of affirming us in our insecurities.

There is a tremendous temptation for us, as women to seek validation from our children because they require so much from us. On the surface, this satisfies our desire to be needed, but it can lead to an unhealthy codependency on those who need us to model dependency on Christ. There's nobody needier than a whiny two-year-old! Mama to the rescue!

However, this unhealthy interconnectedness with our children can begin to affect our marriage because we weren't designed to be our child's *ezer*. This isn't a book on parenting, but it will serve our marriage well if we are able to work with our husbands to steward and shape the child's life entrusted to us for a season, send them off, and find new areas in which we flex our teamwork muscles. It's true that we have a need to be needed, but that is a brilliant design if we can channel that into healthy teamwork in our marriage.

The "S" Word

As much as the Grand Canyon highlighted our tendencies toward danger, one particular hike in Sedona tested my trust in my husband and my ability to hold my tongue. We had heard from friends and read online that one of the most incredible trails and views in the majestic Sedona was at Devil's Bridge.

After an early breakfast at Sedonuts, we were fueled with sugar and excitement when we parked at the trailhead. It was a beautiful morning, and the winding 2.1-mile hike to the largest sandstone arch in the area was pleasant. We played silly games and had sweet conversations with Josie and Colby, occasionally looking ahead, trying to spot our destination. We happily kept moving onward as the path narrowed and turned into rock. The way up proved easy, with only a few places that might call for caution.

Suddenly, I saw it. A line had formed of fellow thrill-seekers waiting to have their picture taken on the narrow strip of rock high above the desert. We had hiked a long way, but the pit in my stomach moved up to my throat and began to settle in as fear. I agreed to stay where I was and take a picture of everything I held dear out on a six-foot-wide arch. Everything in me wanted to dig in my heels and usher my family back down to safety. Only one thing kept me from doing just that—my husband.

We spent the last chapter addressing men and how they should lead their wives by loving and serving them. When a husband is leading and serving his wife well, it makes the directive given to wives in the Ephesians 5:22 much easier to follow: "Wives, submit to your own husbands, as to the Lord. For the husband is the head of the wife even as Christ is the head of the church, his body, and is himself its Savior. Now as the church submits to Christ, so also wives should submit in everything to their husbands."

What?? Wives, submit to your husbands? This passage typically causes women to recoil and cringe worse than I did at the term "helper," but as a woman speaking to women, I want to address a few things that should put your mind at ease.

First, in no way does God's order for the family imply that women are inferior to men. Remember, it speaks to the structure of the family, not to the value of women. Galatians 3:28 tells us that, "There is neither Jew nor Gentile, neither slave nor free, nor is there male and female, for you are all one in Christ Jesus" (NIV). This tells us that all Christians stand on the same footing of son-ship and daughter-ship before God. "We are created equal before God. We stand on the same level ground before him. We are equal in personhood, our being, our worth, but from Genesis-the time of creation- we were given a different role assignment."[3]

Jesus values women and He defied the societal norms of His day by allowing them to sit under His teaching. Mary and Martha were some of His closest friends and the first people Jesus revealed Himself to after the resurrection were women. He loves us deeply. So, I believe that any time scripture, which is inspired by the Lover of our souls, speaks directly to women or wives that it is always going to be for our good, for our protection, and to give us the very best chance to have an abundant life. He designed us and wants us to live our very best lives for His glory.

I understand that the word "submission" may not be a popular one, but it's vital in understanding our relationship with our husbands. Looking at this passage, it tells women to *"submit to your own husbands."* This doesn't say that women need to submit to men in general, nor be a doormat. Notice, it says to "submit to *your own* husband." We are called to yield to the leadership of the man God has chosen for us.

There is great protection for a wife who lives under the authority of a godly man. Women, we must stop buying into the world's view that submission is equated with weakness. That's far from true. Jesus, who had all power and authority submitted His will to the Father in all things. Even Jesus submitted Himself to someone. Are we greater than our Savior, that we are unwilling to trust God's commands for authority? Submission is not weakness. In fact, I believe it takes far greater strength to yield than to clamor for control because it requires humility.

Paul not only tells a wife how she is to act in the relationship with her husband, but it goes a step further and addresses the attitude she is to have as she submits. The action is submission, but her motivation should be to please the Lord. We submit to our husbands *"as unto the Lord."* We serve with a heart that delights in the Lord. We allow Christ to fill us up and we obey Him by loving our husbands God's way, through submission. It's that simple. It's important to understand that this passage does not tell our husbands to *make* us submit to them. This is not an endorsement for the egotistical abuse of power that too often has corrupted how this verse is received. Rather, this submission is given voluntarily, and as seen earlier, it is mutual.

Respect

The second command we are given in our Ephesians 5 passage is to respect our husbands. This is a call to esteem them, hold them in high regard, and honor them. I believe we are given this specific instruction because it's what our man needs most and what is the least natural for us to offer. A man needs to know that the woman beside him admires, respects, and has confidence in his leadership. Without it, he will either wither into passivity or become abusive in his strength. A man who feels highly esteemed and respected by his wife, feels empowered to come through for her. He also desires to love her well. His masculinity is channeled positively for accomplishing his God-ordained mission.

One of the greatest ways we respect our husband, and the hardest, is with our words. It's no secret that women tend to be driven in our relationships to connect through words. It's why we long to sit down and share our hearts with each other through conversations. But if we aren't careful, we can use our words to manipulate rather than encourage and respect our husbands. Instead of offering the life-saving, life giving words that he most needs, we use our words against him. In our attempts to get him to fulfill our desires we resort to nagging and complaining, which leaves our men wounded and emotionally retreating further from us. As your husband's "ezer kenegdo," the lifesaver beside him, God is asking you to offer him life by believing in him and supporting him with both your words and actions.

Leading Up

At this point, I understand that you may be wondering, *what if he's not leading and I have to?* Please hear my heart on this. Through the Holy Spirit's breaking of my pride to realign my thinking with God's word on the matter, I've concluded that He knows best. God did not design wives to live in authority over our husbands. When we put on the mantle that was not suited for us the fit is rather cumbersome. The order that God established for the family becomes disrupted and that authority becomes a heavy burden to bear.

Remember Eve? Adam was with her when she decided to plate dinner from the wrong tree. They were side by side while the serpent tempted her. Adam passively stood by as Eve decided to take matters into her own hands to control her own happiness. She stepped out of line and decided to lead. It didn't turn out so well for her, and I can assure you that it will not profit you to assume your husband's role. It's like stepping into the batter's box as a right-handed hitter and deciding to hit lefty. It's not in your best interest, nor the best interest of your mission.

This doesn't mean you cease to lead altogether. If you have children, you are still called to pour into them spiritually and lead them. You still quietly get up and take them to church on Sundays without huffing and puffing and belittling your husband for sleeping in. If he isn't engaged with your family, you have to step up and keep life moving forward in your household. That's not what I'm talking about. I mean that you can't spiritually lead your husband with your words, nor force him to lead if he's not willing to; that's the role of the Holy Spirit in his life. If he's feeling disrespected by you for not leading the way you want him to, he will associate any talk of God with the bitterness he may have towards you and further withdraw. Scripture says that God's kindness leads us to repentance. I've never heard a man say, "I think I would pull myself together and be everything my wife wants if I can hear just one more lecture!"

So what do you do to encourage your husband to lead your family? Rather than usurp his authority, lead up. God has placed you alongside your husband to be his teammate, to do life with him, to encourage and empower him to be all God has called him to be. Our words are very powerful, but can be a danger to us and our relationship with our husband. This is why 1 Peter 3:1-2 admonishes us, "submit yourselves to your own husbands so that, if any of them do not believe the word, they may be won over without words by the behavior of their wives, when they see the purity and reverence of your lives." Don't step in and attempt to take the authority that God has given your husband. Instead, hold your tongue, submit to him, pray for him, and let your life lead by example.

You may question, *what if I stop leading him and moving us forward and he fails?* Test God with your obedience and see what kind of fruit it yields. What if your controlling is holding him back from thriving? What if your attempts to take the reins keeps your husband from seeing the need to play the man? You've left no room for him to succeed or to be your knight in shining armor if you aren't showing vulnerability. You cannot force your husband to be the leader God has called him to be, but you can empower him and stop standing in his way. Let God deal with his heart. You have enough to manage as you work through this area of learning to submit.

What if you obey God's word and submit to your husband and show him respect and he comes through for you? What if your husband begins to lead you and your family? Then you don't have to carry that weight anymore. Our attempts to control our spouse exposes our lack of trust in the God who has a better plan for us than we can manipulate for ourselves. We will never walk in this peace if we don't first obey.

As a small child, I witnessed this kind of submission and respect transform my family. Since my Daddy passed away, I have pieced together long forgotten memories with snippets of stories from my Mama. My parents' marriage is one of the truly beautiful love stories, but it didn't start out that way. When my parents got married at age nineteen, they weren't living by God's design. My Daddy didn't know Jesus. My Mama was a believer, but wasn't walking closely with the Lord. They were young and had very little direction in marriage.

Being married at such a young age, Daddy was still a boy in a grown man's body, often selfish and unaware of the leadership his young wife and three small children needed. I can still remember weekends when he would go away on hunting trips with his friends, leaving my Mama with my sister, brother, and me at our home on the farm. I have vague memories of him hitting his hand with a hammer and letting out a couple of words that we would have gotten a spanking for saying, but I barely remember that Daddy now.

God started drawing Mama back to Himself when I was little. Though Daddy wasn't interested in church, he was okay with Mama taking us on Sundays. The four of us prayed many nights that he would come to know Jesus.

During that time, Mama joined a ladies Bible study group. That group changed her life and saved her marriage before her growing resentment turned to bitterness. She said that as frustrated as she was, God began to speak to her heart about following His design for the relationship. Rather than nagging Daddy to get him to do what she wanted, she began doing what felt counterintuitive. She prayed, served, and submitted.

My Daddy had quite a few hunting dogs back in the day and he kept them in a dog pen that sat maybe fifty feet from our back door. On hot, muggy days, we would catch a whiff of the smell coming from the pen, if Daddy hadn't hosed it out in a while. It was a source of contention for my parents, and Mama said she repeatedly asked for it to be handled.

One day, as my Daddy was headed back in town from one of his weekend hunting trips, Mama said she felt the Lord dealing with her attitude toward him and breaking her. She said she put on some old boots, went out to that pen, and started shoveling poop and hosing down the concrete floor. After she finished, she cleaned herself up and started cooking Daddy's favorite meal. Even though she was tired and felt overlooked, she decided to only use words that would affirm her husband when he walked through the door.

She said he looked a bit stunned when he came in the house after putting his dogs back in their pen before coming inside for supper. Daddy had noticed the clean dog pen. When asked about it, Mama didn't pat herself on the back, nor remind him of how long he had neglected the chore, nor make him feel bad for his time away. Mama served Daddy like she was serving Jesus. That night she felt him take an ever so slight step toward her, so she took another towards him, and another.

I will never forget the night that my Daddy walked down the aisle of our church and publicly confessed that he had given his life to Jesus. Over the next ten years that I lived at home, and after, the memories I had of my Daddy cursing out of frustration were replaced by memories of his leadership. I barely recall a morning after my Daddy decided to follow Jesus that I didn't see him sitting over his Bible at breakfast, then eventually pouring over lessons as he became a deacon and a Sunday school teacher in our church. He became a godly man and leader of our family.

It all started when my Mama relinquished the leadership role, showed Daddy respect he had not yet earned, and submitted out of obedience to the Lord. She chose to trust God's plan for her marriage over her own attempts to fix it.

My parents were married close to fifty years before my Daddy was killed unexpectedly in an accident on our family farm. The tragedy of it all is that Mama said they were enjoying their golden years together. Though Daddy wasn't perfect, he had become the man of Mama's dreams. They had learned to love and respect each other through years of working together to raise three children, who all love the Lord. They enjoyed the time they spent together working and playing on the farm they called home. Their reliance on the Lord, their common mission, and teamwork had yielded a sweet season of intimate friendship.

CHAPTER 8:

WORKING TOGETHER

Any time you take a family vacation, there are a lot of things that must get done, especially when it involves an RV, kids, a dog, and almost 4,000 miles of driving! Over the years, Bonnie and I have learned how to work together pretty well. After all, we literally worked side by side 24/7 for twenty years. Our cross-country trip was no different.

A trip of this magnitude required us to flex our teamwork muscles. While I am good at many things, others escape the realm of my skill set. Items on that list would be navigation, cooking, and remembering to remove the Wi-Fi antenna from the top of the RV before driving! Non-flexible antennas don't stand a chance against low hanging tree limbs. I have long since learned that I rely on Bonnie for many things, but reminding me about that antenna tops the list. Similarly, Bonnie claims that she isn't good at emptying the sewage tanks on the RV. I guess we all have our gifts.

By the last leg of our journey, we had become quite fluid with our dance of packing up to head out for the day. I prepared the exterior for departure. Crank the motor home engine-Check. Take off the trash- Check. Unplug power and water- Check. Take down that pesky Wi-Fi antenna outside. Got it!

Meanwhile, Bonnie went through her interior check-list. Drain the faucets, latch the shower and bathroom doors, pull back the rear window curtains for visibility, take down the privacy curtain, bolt down or remove anything that could fall. We had our roles and worked together to keep us on schedule for our daily adventures!

Roles

Have you ever had the opportunity to play, or at least watch a team sport? Whether it is soccer, softball, football, or volleyball, a team's mission is typically the same, to win a championship! Successful coaches will cast the vision for getting there by breaking down a season into individual attainable game by game goals. Then he studies opponents and designs practices and drills to help his team tackle one opponent at a time. However, a team can practice as much as they want and never win a game if they aren't able to work together on game-day. Winning is also unlikely if the team is stacked with players who have the same strengths and weaknesses. Team sports require players to have unique positional skills and stay in their lanes.

When God gave man his part of the mission, we see that he was alone in the garden. Woman had not been created yet. After He delivered Adam his greatest gift, Eve, and all their combined strengths had been unified, God addressed them as a couple and sent them out on their common mission. We believe it speaks to the fact that by God's design, husbands and wives each have unique assets to bring to the marriage, and it takes both of them to accomplish their mission.

Ecclesiastes 4:9 reinforces the idea that God intends for us to accomplish more together than apart. "Two are better than one, because they have a good return for their labor" (NIV). God saw Adam's weaknesses and filled the gaps with Eve. God knew where Adam was already fully capable and didn't see the need to duplicate those roles in his wife.

God has created all of us with specific strengths, talents, personalities, and passions; that, too, was by design. It shouldn't at this point in our lives, but it still amazes us to see how different husbands and wives are from each other. As we lead premarital workshops and married couple workshops, it is truly rare to find people who are married to someone exactly like themselves. The great news is that each spouse brings individualism and unique abilities into the marriage. Though differences are often a source of conflict in relationships, couples can thrive when they are willing to view them as complementary traits that strengthen their team. Just think, if you were exactly alike there would be no need for one of you!

Remember the story about Colby's first season playing baseball? Well, that year Colby had the opportunity to learn so much about every position on the field. In that first season, instead of putting kids in a fixed position, his coaches rotated players around the field and every kid got to try playing every position. This was actually a great idea. Colby had the opportunity to learn about every baseball position and began to see that each position had a unique role and responsibility on the team. Once kids are put into fixed positions, they are usually placed there because of the way they are gifted. A taller kid might play first base, a quicker kid may play shortstop. If a kid has a strong arm, he's going to play third base, and the toughest kid usually plays catcher. The coach's kid is always the pitcher... I'm just kidding!

In marriage, we find the roles that we each play the best and play them. There's just no need for two first basemen! Each couple has to determine together how relationship responsibilities should be distributed based on what best serves their team. Some women may actually love doing yard work and men may be incredible in the kitchen. Oftentimes husbands feel responsible for making all financial decisions and handling the checkbook and paying bills. I (Daniel) am not one of them since my math skills are limited to counting on my fingers and toes (and I'm missing one of those)! In fact, before I got married, one of the qualifications my parents had for my future spouse was that she be able to balance a checkbook. Lucky for me, Bonnie is good at math!

Now, I could attempt to keep our finances and get us into a bit of a jam, or we can budget and set financial goals together, and I can allow Bonnie to use her abilities to manage the details. However, it would not serve our marriage well for Bonnie to keep the finances if she has an addiction to clicking the "buy now" button on Amazon. You have to assess your individual strengths and weaknesses and work them to your advantage.

> Listen to *The Marriage Adventure Podcast, Episode 27* to learn about working as a team when it comes to household chores. www.themarriageadventure.com/podcasts

Playing "Back-Up"

I have a confession to make, I hate driving. Daniel seems to enjoy it and can look out that windshield for hours on end, only stopping for gas and bathroom breaks. But on our cross-country road trip, it became necessary for my weary husband to move out of the driver's seat to rest; It was in the best interest of everyone in the vehicle. On those occasions, I had to suck up my preference for the passenger seat and take the wheel.

It's a beautiful thing in marriage when both spouses operate in their giftedness and enjoy their assignment, but it doesn't always work out that way. Keep in mind that the functional roles we play may change depending on our season of life.

When I delivered our daughter via cesarean section, I temporarily suspended my cooking and cleaning duties. Daniel stepped in and took care of the majority of the housework until I was able to contribute again. Walking through seasons of life that require us to play a team position that is not our favorite, or isn't in our primary gifting, requires us to draw from the source of strength we can find only in our walk with Christ. It's a call to, "Clothe yourselves, all of you, with humility toward one another, for God opposes the proud but gives grace to the humble"(1 Pet. 5:5).

We don't always get to play our favorite position on the team, but we must be willing to play where there are holes to fill. Sometimes we have to give up our wants to do what's best for the team. There will be times we are called on to play undesirable roles in our family dynamic. Who wants to unload the dishwasher, vacuum, pull weeds, change diapers, wash the car, and help with homework? Those tasks are not fun, but needed. If it's where the balls are being hit, get out there and field them.

God calls us to back up our spouse, both physically and emotionally. When our spouse drops the ball, is unavailable, or simply needs help, we are there to back them up, to fill the gap, per se. They need to be able to count on us to physically come through for them. Even more importantly, our spouse needs to know that we will provide emotional support when needed. As a mother, I experience this daily when I'm exhausted from being the repetitive voice our children have learned to tune out by eight o'clock at night. I can always count on Daniel to be the fresh voice that gets their attention and obedience. Even if we don't agree with each other in a moment of parenting, I can trust that we will make a united stand in front of our children and then when we're alone together, say, "Umm, can we chat about what just happened?"

We need to be able to back each other up in the routines of everyday life because it builds trust and security for the times when we find ourselves completely benched for entire games, not just single innings. I don't think I have ever felt more emotionally supported, nor needed it more, than when I experienced the sudden loss of my Daddy in 2012. Daniel took the phone call from my brother, then had to tell me that my sixty-two-year-old dad had lost his life in an accident on our family farm.

In the weeks and months that followed, I felt paralyzed. Daniel stepped in and physically handled not only his normal roles but also covered most of mine, which included the care of one-and-a-half and three-and-a-half-year-old toddler. If I cooked or cleaned once in a three-week period, I don't remember it. And what's more, Daniel's emotional support carried me through the darkest days I had experienced to that point in my life. Was that season easy for Daniel? I doubt it, but I never would have known it. He played the positions that were most needed and moved our home team through the crisis. You never know when you might be called on to back up your spouse, but being willing and prepared to do so provides stability and strength to carry you through difficult times.

Pulling Your Own Weight

Since movies were still a few years from being invented, Jesus taught many lessons through parables. In Matthew 25:14-30, Jesus shares the parable of the talents. In this parable, He tells about a man who went on a journey and before he left, he entrusted his servants with varying amounts of money (talents). When we returned, he was anxious to see how each servant used or invested the money.

In the same way, God has uniquely gifted you and your spouse. But why is it that so often we see a marriage with two uniquely gifted people have difficulties handling the routine ups and downs of life? Many times, it's because one spouse isn't being a good steward of his/her talents.

At Christmas time, we have a little manger scene that sits in our front yard. These plastic replicas of Mary and Joseph are special to us because they used to belong to our elderly neighbor across the street. When Josie was little, she would walk into their yard and sit with the little lamb and talk to the plastic baby Jesus. Sometimes she'd pick him up and rock him. Now that Josie is older and wiser, she is more attuned to what's happening. This past Christmas, as we were pulling out of the driveway, she noticed that Joseph had blown over in the wind. She quickly said, "Joseph, you better stop sleeping on the job! Get up and help Mary with that baby!"

Just like plastic Mary and Joseph, many marriages have one person sleeping on the job. Sometimes this happens because of laziness. One mate gets used to having a "house-keeper," or they might get caught up in a hobby. It can also occur because of a feeling of inadequacy. When a new baby arrives, the new mom seems way more natural with the baby, so the new dad starts to disconnect.

Whatever the case may be, marriages need a balance of ownership. Both the husband and the wife must be proactive in the relationship. Like Jesus' parable illustrated, we should use and invest our talents and skills to help move our family's team forward. Teams get bogged down when one or several teammates don't step up and play to their potential.

One question we have found to be very helpful in our relationship is, "How can I help?" This proactivity allows us to be partners or teammates in the relationship. Also, taking turns bathing the kids, folding laundry, or grocery shopping gives us more time to relax together (or separate). It also helps keep one spouse from getting resentful from having to carry the entire load. Reaching God-sized missions in our marriage requires both spouses to carry their own load.

Team Evaluation

As we mentioned earlier, during our 20s, we traveled full time on the road leading worship. If there's one bit of advice I would go back and give my younger self, it would be to invest in a tire pressure gauge and use it! I remember replacing seven tires in one year! Not because they were old or low on tread, but because I was an idiot and didn't take care of them.

When we purchased The Hoover Mover, the first thing I bought was a Tire Pressure Monitor System or TPMS for short. If you have a vehicle that was built anytime in this century, it's probably standard, but The Hoover Mover was not of this century. It is from days gone by. What does a TPMS do? In simple terms, it measures the pressure and temperature of my tires. Then it sends the information back to a little digital box that sits conveniently on my dashboard. When we left town on our cross-country trip, I filled the tires with air. Then, as we traveled, I could conveniently and consistently evaluate them from the comfort of my captain's chair as we drove. Guess what? We didn't have any flat tires. Brilliant!

One thing that great teams do is continually evaluate. What is working? What's not working? How can something be done more efficiently or effectively? These are principles that we should bring into our family. Sometimes things may be working well. However, as the seasons of life change, we may need to reevaluate.

For twenty-four years, I have handled the yard work. To be honest, it's not my favorite, but I'm the man. I'm not going to make my poor wife get out and cut the grass, trim shrubbery, and pull weeds. Then 2020 hit and the kids began digital learning at home. After several months, Bonnie came to me and asked if she could cut the grass and take over the yard work. While most men would think this was foreplay, I was somewhat offended. Was I not doing a good enough job (probably not, but that's another story)? When I heard Bonnie out, I swallowed my man-pride, and we adjusted our roles. My introverted wife explained that she wanted to get outside after so much togetherness because she needed some alone time, and she was confident the kids wouldn't follow her out there to do yard work!

Even knowing this was something my wife needed, I still had an internal struggle. A couple of discussions led us to reevaluate a few tasks. Based on our likes, dislikes, gifts, and needs, we adjusted several jobs and assignments to create better teamwork.

When was the last time you and your spouse sat down and evaluated how well you work together as a team? Maybe you've been holding on to a task your spouse could accomplish in half the time out of pride. Perhaps your efforts would serve your team better elsewhere. Here's what we'd like to propose.

Schedule a date night or an evening at home to sit down and evaluate your strengths and weaknesses. Take into account your personalities, passions, and available time. Remember, you may not love every role you are required to play, but covering every area is the best way to make sure you are moving toward your mission.

> Visit www.themarriageadventure.com/team-worksheet to download a free pdf worksheet to create a plan for working together as a team.

Team Evaluation Exercise

1. Make a list of all of the tasks and chores required that have to be accomplished each week/ month. (Budgeting/ Bill Paying/ Meal Planning/ Shopping/ Cooking/ Calendar Management/ Household Chores/ Date nights/ Child Care/ Child Extracurricular Activities, Etc.)
2. Prioritize. Obviously, things like meal planning/ prep and paying bills will be pretty high on the list. (Ya gotta eat and you don't want your lights turned off!)
3. List each person's current responsibilities.
4. List the things that nobody owns but have to get done. Add the things that aren't currently getting done.
5. Cross off anything on the list that is unnecessary.
6. What do you LOVE? Put a star and your initial next to it.
7. What do you dread? Put an X and your initial next to it.

8. Discuss your love/dread list and see if there is anything that you immediately wouldn't mind trading or owning.
9. Is there any responsibility you can swap based on interest or giftedness? Some may be obvious if you can do it in minutes and it takes your spouse hours.
10. Discuss the items that you both hate. What tasks are you willing to take over that would serve your spouse?
11. What tasks do you need to give up that would better serve your marriage?
12. How should we adjust what we are currently doing for the good of the team?

CHAPTER 9:

BREAKING PATTERNS

"**I**t's not your lucky day."

That's never a good thing to hear when you're on vacation. While in Sedona, we had the most fabulous morning. We had a great breakfast, then a fascinating hike to see the Birthing Cave. You can use your imagination as to why it's called that. Afterward, we got in our rental car and headed to our next attraction. That's when it happened. I saw those dreaded blue lights in the rearview mirror.

Being unfamiliar with the area, I honestly hadn't noticed that the speed limit changed from 55 to 35 miles per hour. I was going about my business and driving the speed I was accustomed to in Georgia, but that didn't matter to the lady officer who stood outside the rental car holding my license.

"Sir, this is a school zone, and I'm here to enforce a penalty that will break bad driving habits." She did so by giving me a $350 speeding ticket.

Ruts

I love a good southern accent. Both of us grew up in Georgia where elongated syllables roll off the tongues of country girls like sugar drips from iced tea. My military family planted in Warner Robins, Georgia, when I was five years old. It was a melting pot of servicemen and women from all over the United States, so I didn't really have much of a southern drawl. But Bonnie's accent was so thick when we met that some of her words needed interpreting.

Where did Bonnie get her accent? My "country girl" grew up in the country! Bonnie lived out in the middle of nowhere that you had to take miles of dirt roads to get to. When I first drove to her house, I thought that eventually I'd have to park, then swing on vines the rest of the way! Having learned to drive on those red clay roads, Bonnie learned to navigate around the ruts that would form after it rained and then dried. It might be weeks before the county would send out equipment to drag the ditches, scrape the dirt up, and flatten it back down to make the roads smooth again. It didn't take long for more ruts to form after driving over it day after day.

When we were dating, I was driving Bonnie's little sports car on the unpaved road that led to her house one rainy afternoon. She warned me about the ruts in the road that the torrential downpour had caused. Needless to say, an hour later, her daddy finally got the car out of the ditch that I had accidentally parked it in.

In marriage, we can know where we're going, be working together to get there, but not be making progress because we have gotten into unhealthy ruts in our relationship. Moving forward may call for behavior modification to break bad habits and reshape the way you have been relating to each other in your marriage. After all, working together as a team involves communication and conflict resolution. Most married couples have destructive patterns and habits when it comes to these exact areas.

Patterns can be a lot like ruts on a dirt road. Our marriage often ends up in the ditch because of the harmful patterns and habits we allow ourselves to live in that have been formed over time. Because these patterns are ingrained, it's difficult for us to begin realigning and orienting our family's activities, finances, and interests to our new common mission. Before we can work together effectively, we may have to break some bad patterns before we end up in a ditch or with a hefty fine for speeding along our adventure.

"That Stupid Test"

We can develop healthy teamwork in our marriages, but there are many unhealthy patterns to break along the way, whether we realize it or not. Several years ago, Bonnie and I went through training to become facilitators for a well-known premarital and marriage enrichment assessment. In doing so, we had to take the marital assessment. It's about three hundred questions long and took us about thirty minutes to complete. We might have been a little cocky. Okay, we pretty much assumed we would score higher than any other couple... ever. We were wrong! Because of the initial conflict that followed, we started calling it "that stupid test!"

Our scores were good; however, one area stood out. Do you remember when you were a kid, and you brought a report card home that had all A's and one C-? That's basically what happened. When it comes to resolving conflict, we got a C-. The following year, the company came out with a new product. We took that assessment and got the same results. We were astonished. One test might be a fluke, but not two. I looked at Bonnie and said, "How are you answering these questions? Do you really feel this way?" Bonnie squinched her nose and reluctantly nodded her head yes. She said that sometimes she struggles with having a voice in our relationship. Wow! Her answer truly broke my heart. After eighteen years of marriage, we became aware of some unhealthy patterns in our relationship that needed breaking. We now had a new common mission, to take the information we had in front of us and fix this.

Here's what you have to understand, Bonnie and I don't argue much. We might disagree sometimes, but rarely does it end up in conflict. Now we knew why; it was literally in black and white. On the assessment, Bonnie scored very low on assertiveness and high on avoidance, meaning she doesn't often like to assert her opinion or feelings. She also doesn't like conflict and will avoid it at any cost. Since Bonnie didn't speak up, I would assume she agreed with me on the particular subject. On the rare occasion when she did voice her opinion, I would use my "humor and charm" to politely talk her into my way of thinking.

What I was actually doing was manipulating her. I wasn't mean or forceful about it, but without knowing it, I was bulldozing her. This left her without a voice in the relationship. How did we break this pattern we had formed over almost twenty years? It took intentionality and a lot of work.

It wasn't too long after that Bonnie wanted to renovate our kitchen. Luckily, there aren't any dead mice involved in this story. On a project like this, similar to the motorhome story, I would lead the charge with vision and direction, and Bonnie would help. However, since this was her idea (and I love to eat her cooking), I realized it needed to be her kitchen project. When she brought the idea to me, she already had a Pinterest board and tons of ideas.

As I tried to insert my thoughts, Bonnie was armed and ready. She politely said, "Nope. I prefer to do it this way."

What? Who is this woman? Her newfound voice was kind of attractive. As we laid flooring, painted, hung shiplap, and built shelves, I found myself as the helper while Bonnie drove the project forward. Our kitchen renovation provided an excellent opportunity for us to begin to break out of the rut we had been in all those years. Since then, we've worked hard to make sure we both have a voice in the relationship.

Sometimes it takes years to form harmful relational patterns, so don't expect to break them by merely becoming aware of them. God changes our hearts with His truth, but we have to allow Him to bring our actions in alignment with that truth. Why is this difficult? It's because of these deep-seated patterns we have developed for how we live life.

From the time we were children, we have learned ways to communicate and deal with the world around us. Why did Bonnie have a difficult time expressing her opinions? She grew up with an assertive dad who had no problem making decisions for her family, and she became accustomed to submitting to her dad's leadership.

I, on the other hand, was used to asserting my ideas and fighting for them. As the youngest of four boys, I had been conditioned by the motto, "if you don't grab, you don't get." So, I had learned to contend for what I wanted. Over time, Bonnie's people-pleasing, conflict-hating personality settled into going with the flow. It didn't seem worth a fight to find her voice. Unfortunately, my assertiveness and her lack of it, led to habitual unhealthy conflict resolution in our relationship.

Whether good or bad, patterns will eventually take shape and become ingrained. Depending on our environment, we may have established healthy habits, but more often, we develop unhealthy methods for handling communication, conflict resolution, financial management, etc. Once instilled, these are difficult to break, but it's not impossible!

> Listen to *The Marriage Adventure Podcast,*
> *Episode 35* to learn some lessons from
> newlyweds and see if you've developed
> some bad patterns over the years. www.
> themarriageadventure.com/podcasts

Recognizing Patterns

Before we can ever begin to function as a team in our marriage, we must be willing to recognize the patterns we've developed that directly oppose teamwork. Many couples fall into the trap of negative communication that eventually leads to pulling away from each other. They engage in more "win/lose" conversations than in issue-based discussions. A thought process directs the way they communicate with each other. *If I give in to my spouse in this scenario, then I lose, and they win.* This type of thinking pits couples against each other as opponents rather than teammates. If we are going to operate as a team, we must first remember that we are a team and working toward a common goal.

Iconic women's basketball coach, Pat Summit, who coached thirty-eight seasons at the University of Tennessee and won more games than any other coach in college basketball history, man or woman, understood the importance of teamwork. She said, "Teamwork is recognizing that your personal ambitions and the ambitions of the team are one and the same."[1] She also said, "Teamwork causes common people to obtain uncommon results."[2] Before we can ever reach the common mission we've set for our marriage and family, we must make sure we are a team and break the destructive patterns that have been holding us back from working together in our marriage.

How do you break a negative or harmful pattern? Typically, a habit or routine must be interacted upon by an outside force of some kind. One of our favorite TV shows used to be, *The Biggest Loser*. On this show, contestants, usually weighing more than 300 or 400 pounds, would compete to see who could lose the most weight. I remember thinking, *why would anyone sign up to go on national TV to take their shirt off and endure ridicule. Don't they have a local trainer and Weight Watchers?* By that point, I'm sure they had probably tried everything they could on their own. What the TV show offered them was something out-side of their norm. It provided an outside force that consisted of accountability, coaching, and financial reward that they could not obtain alone.

To break a pattern, we have to put something in place that is so uncomfortable that it will force change. With my speeding in Sedona, the thing that slowed me down was a four-hour online driving course that reduced my $350 speeding ticket to $200. Typically, in marriage, so many of our negative patterns and habits revolve around communication and conflict resolution. Since hundreds of books have been written on those topics, we won't dive into them directly, but the concepts are the same. To take steps away from harmful patterns toward healthy ones that put us back on the same team, we must have two things: accountability and coaching.

Accountability

In marriage, accountability can come from your spouse, but it is often necessary to seek it from an ongoing, unbiased, trustworthy person outside of your relationship. However, some rules should be in place. First and foremost, accountability must come from a person of the same sex as you. Never talk to someone of the opposite sex about your marriage. You are asking for trouble.

We have a rule. I don't have female friends, and Bonnie doesn't have male friends. I have one female friend... I married her. Besides my wife, I have a relationship with my mom and daughter. Co-workers are just that, co-workers. Relationships with co-workers must remain professional. Be very careful here.

Another guideline for accountability is the person you seek it from must be a godly friend, emphasizing *godly*. This person isn't someone that you only vent your problems to, but is someone who can take you to scripture, look you in the eye, and tell you the truth. I (Bonnie) have a friend I've been meeting with to study the Bible for the past fifteen years. She points me to the truth and encourages growth in my marriage, so I trusted her counsel as she walked with me during Daniel's forty-year-old pit, which we spoke about earlier. She gave me some valuable advice that challenged me and changed my entire understanding of my marriage relationship for the better.

Third, it's unwise to seek accountability in marriage issues from family members because they rarely have the ability to offer unbiased counsel. If they do provide unbiased counsel, it can often hurt the family relationship. When we were planning to get married, both of our parents gave us this advice. My mom said, "Bonnie, I'm giving you away, and I don't want you back. When you and Daniel have an argument or a fight, you don't need to tell me about it. You'll forgive him and move on, but I won't. I'll hold it against him forever."

As much as they wanted to continue to be our confidants, our parents understood that they were prone to take sides in the conflict. To this day, my (Daniel's) parents probably think Bonnie is perfect. Honestly, they probably like her more than they like me!

External accountability might feel natural, but how does it come from within the spousal relationship? For this to occur, both of you must be willing participants. If one of you hasn't invited this level of accountability, the other will perceive it as bossy, nagging, or bullying. This type of accountability requires both of you to have a common language to express your desires in the relationship. This comes from reading the same books (maybe this one), going to workshops, attending marriage retreats, listening to podcasts, etc. Then, when you are on a date or having pillow talk, discuss what you learned; talk about your relationship. I know, guys, that's not the way we're wired, but sometimes, we need to be open to rewiring.

One thing to remember, when you try to hold each other accountable, do so in a way that is respectful and kind. Assert yourself, but be kind, gentle, and full of grace. Communicate with each other in such a way that brings clarity and understanding to the situation. The last thing you want is for your spouse to put up a wall and feel attacked. "Only about 7% of all communication is based on words and the meanings of those words. Nonverbal body language covers 55%, and your tone of voice the other 38%. This means that *how* you express yourself is five to eight times louder than *what* you have to say. It can be very easy to misread and misinterpret someone, thereby creating additional tension and conflict that derails the process."[3]

If this is true, imagine sitting in the car with your spouse, and you want them to listen to something you recently heard on a podcast. You begin playing that message through the speaker of your smartphone. However, at the same time, your local country music station is blaring through the car stereo system. Which message will they hear, the one that is turned up to 55% or 7%? When communicating with your spouse, you must get the message across in a way that they can hear and understand, not just the way you want to say it.

As passionate as you might be about a subject and as pure as your motives may be, learning to communicate in a way that your spouse can receive it will allow you to walk in genuine accountability with each other and will increase intimacy. If we are going to function as teammates rather than opponents, we must be open to accountability as we break harmful patterns.

Coaching

As mentioned earlier, we spent many years traveling around singing and leading worship. Singing day after day for weeks on end requires good technique. You may not know this, but as with anything else, there is a proper way to sing that gives your voice quality (pitch, tone, and range) and sustainability. I thought that I was a good singer as a teenager. One of my part-time jobs in high school was as a wedding singer, not exactly like the movie, but it was close.

I'll never forget when I got to my first college vocal lesson. Half-way through, my professor looked at me and said, "Daniel, talent will only take you so far, and then you have to work hard. You're there." For the next four years, my vocal professor kicked my rear-end, breaking all the bad habits I had grown accustomed to and teaching me how to sing correctly. Boy, did it pay off! For the next twenty years, I made my living benefiting from that hard work.

Sometimes you need a coach to come alongside you in life or in your marriage to help you break negative patterns. Proverbs 12:15 says, "The way of a fool is right in his own eyes, but a wise man listens to advice." What does coaching look like? Coaching can come in many forms. It may be as simple as signing up for a class. There are tons of online workshops and classes available for couples to attend together. As mentioned above, listening to podcasts and reading books can provide a degree of relationship coaching.

For more direct coaching, you may want to seek out a pastoral counselor. If your church doesn't have one, certainly there is a church around you that does. I'm not only the Executive Pastor at NorthStar Church, but I'm also a pastoral counselor. Pastoral counseling is usually short-term (3-4 sessions) and free. However, if you need more in-depth and extended coaching, it would be a good idea to seek out licensed professional counseling or discipleship counseling from a local agency (your church should be able to point you in the right direction).

As you work to break bad patterns in your marriage, don't get discouraged if you don't start winning games together immediately. Any good marriage coach can help you understand what good sports coaches know; practice and repetition are the keys to creating habits that lead to victory over time. It may take months, even years, to undo the selfish routines that have become so comfortable in your relationship, but the more you both work together to move toward health, the more natural it becomes. Then, before long, you will start noticing that there's a payoff. Celebrate even the smallest victories when you recognize how much better you are working as a unit.

Teammates

Once we are able to recognize and embrace the structure of our team and the unique roles we are designed to play, we are better equipped to work as teammates to fulfill the common mission we've been called to. God fully intends for husbands and wives to learn to put aside their selfishness and work together in harmony.

"Therefore, a man shall leave his father and mother and hold fast to his wife, and the two shall become one flesh" (Eph. 5:31). We hold fast to each other. We become one flesh. We operate in unity as teammates rather than opponents. No team wins when it is in constant turmoil within itself and fighting over who plays what position. The marriage relationship is similar to the church. We are one body with different parts; if one of us wins, we both win.

God's design for the roles we play as teammates is far better than ours. Scripture seems to hit the nail on the head when addressing what we are to offer each other in the marriage relationship. Women are admonished to voluntarily give the one thing that their husbands most need, but comes least natural to give... respect. Men are told to shower their wives with what they most desire, but isn't typically on a man's mind...love.

Interestingly enough, the common, and very clear directive to both husbands and wives, the glue that binds them together, is what comes least natural to both. We are told to serve each other. As we lay down our own desires and serve, we become teammates who can accomplish far more together than apart for the glory of God.

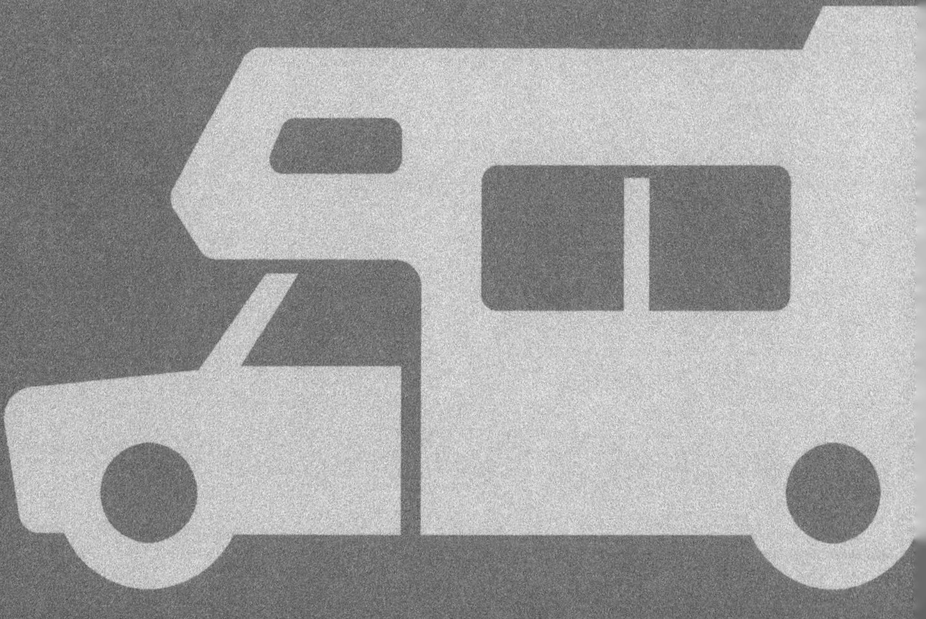

CHAPTER 10:

FRIENDSHIP FACTOR

After driving 1,800 miles in four days, we pulled into the Grand Canyon campground around 10pm on Christmas Eve. We were all excited to wake up on Christmas morning and open the gifts that took up almost our entire kitchen and living room in the Hoover Mover. Eating Bonnie's homemade cinnamon rolls was the only tradition that stayed intact on this COVID Christmas morning, so far from home.

Mid-morning, we cleaned up our tiny home on wheels, bundled up, strapped on our backpacks, and caught a shuttle over to the visitor's center. Bonnie and I visited the Grand Canyon together years ago, but we couldn't wait to see the look on Josie's and Colby's face when they saw it for the first time. I ran ahead of my little crew to get in place with the video camera so I could capture their initial reaction. When they rounded the corner and laid eyes on one of the seven natural wonders of the world, all they could say was, "Wow!"

That word was repeated at almost every overlook for the rest of our day hike at the Grand Canyon. My heart was full as I stood there with my family taking in the majestic views from the rim. That's when I flashed back to a phone call I received from a buddy two decades ago. My friend's job had taken him to

Colorado, and he had a free afternoon to spend how-ever he wanted. I'll never forget hearing something sad in his voice as he told me he was calling from the Rocky Mountains. "This place is so beautiful, and I just needed to call someone to share it with me."

After months of dreaming and planning, I took a moment to breathe in the cold canyon air and enjoy the experience. I can't explain the satisfaction and exhilaration of standing there, fully aware of the memory I was locking in with my best friend. Bonnie's eyes locked on mine for a few brief seconds as we smiled and exchanged the unspoken words, "We did it! We're finally here!"

Super Glue

Great things can be accomplished when a team is inspired by a vision and works together toward a sin-gular mission! What kind of things? Well, with a World Series Championship as the "bulls-eye" on the wall, the 1991 Braves was the only team in MBL history to go from worst to first in a single season.

With the simple mission of "Be America's best quick-service restaurant," a single Dwarf House restaurant opened in 1946. In 2020, it was voted the third most popular fast-food restaurant in America, with more than 2300 restaurants. You know it as Chick-fil-A.

In September 1620, 102 passengers left Plymouth, England, on a small ship dreaming it would carry them to a better life of land ownership and religious freedom. After enduring many hardships and losses, our founding fathers established a little republic that stands almost 250 years later as the beacon of light and liberty for the world, the United States of America.

In 1962, President John F. Kennedy challenged our nation with the mission of sending a man to the moon.

With this grand vision laid before them, over 400,000 people combined their intellect, ingenuity, and passion over the next seven years. On July 20th, 1969, breathless citizens tuned in from earth to hear the iconic words spoken by astronaut Neil Armstrong as the first man to step foot on the moon, "That's one small step for man, one giant leap for mankind."

It's incredible what a team of people can accomplish when they work together! Any community or corporation can share values and goals and reach a mission, but this is marriage we are talking about. What sets a husband and wife apart from any other kind of team? It's the fact that they are bonded together as intimate friends.

Have you ever used superglue? I used some just last night. As we were sitting in our (mice free) RV writing this book, the knob on my air conditioner fell off. It always falls off. I usually ignore it and stick it back on, knowing that it's just going to fall off again. Last night I had enough. I reached over about a foot from where I was sitting, opened the kitchen drawer, and pulled out the tube of super glue. Guess what? Now, when I drive down bumpy roads on our adventures, it won't fall off!

Intimate friendship is a bonding agent, just like super glue. It makes the rough times more manageable by keeping our hearts soft towards each other, and it makes the good times more meaningful.

It's Not Good for Man to Be Alone

One Fourth of July holiday, my (Bonnie's) extended family gathered together at my aunt's farmhouse to spend some time together catching up. The grown-ups spent a full, hot day eating and chatting with siblings and cousins. We also watched the thirteen grandchildren play baseball in the yard, swim in the pool, and run around the yard having fun. When darkness came upon us, the men took the big boys and the fireworks over to the clearing next to the house. They were ready to light up the sky. The boys were having a blast, but I was a nervous wreck worrying about all the little pyromaniacs huddled over the explosives. That's when I looked at my sister and said, "I think this is why God said, 'it's not good for man to be alone!'"

We're pretty sure God didn't create women because He thought men needed supervision. Someone recently asked us, "you know why God created man first? Because he didn't need a woman telling him how to do it."

Seriously though, God knew exactly what He was doing. Even though Adam had a conversational, unbroken relationship with God, something was missing. There is a tendency to believe that women are far more relational than men, and maybe it does come more naturally to them. But God looked around at every good thing He had created and knew that whether Adam acknowledged it or not, nothing in existence could fill man's need for physical and emotional human companionship. How sad for Adam to have the task of naming all the animals on earth and have nobody to turn to and say, "Look how cool that animal with a long neck is. Let's call it a giraffe! Wow! Look at the brilliance of that sunset!" Or, "See how tall that tree is? Watch me climb it!" We all desire to share our experiences with someone who can appreciate them as much as we do. And that's how most relationships begin...with friendship.

Remember when the two of you were dating? Courtship was the exhilarating adventure of determining compatibility. The physical attraction then led to countless hours together. The more time you spent together, your hearts bound through shared experiences. You explored mutual hobbies, discovered common passions and goals, and then bonded over hopes and dreams for the future. C.S. Lewis expresses it this way in His book, *The Four Loves*:

> Friendship arises out of mere companionship when two or more of the companions discover that they have in common some insight or interest or even taste which the others do not share and which, till that moment, each believed to be his unique treasure (or burden). The typical expression of opening friendship would be something like, "What? You too? I thought I was the only one."

> When two such persons discover one another, when, whether with immense difficulties and semi-articulate fumblings or with what would seem to us incredible and elliptical speed, they share their vision- it is then that friendship is born. And instantly, they stand together in an immense solitude.[1]

I'll never forget the first time I saw Bonnie. That memory is forever etched in my mind. I HAD to meet this beautiful girl. After I admired her from a distance for a week or two (no, I didn't stalk her...much), a mutual friend introduced us casually in the student center of our small Christian college. One of the most defining nights of my life came a few weeks later.

We had been on a few casual dates. Then it happened. We had "the conversation." On a Sunday evening, we went out to a river near our college and walked out on the abandoned train trestles overlooking the moonlit water. We sat on those trestles and talked for about four hours under the stars. It was magical. It had to be magic because we've gone back since then and feared for our lives!

That evening we shared our stories and our future hopes and dreams. At one point, I had to be aware of how descriptive I was getting because I felt like I was describing Bonnie. That was the start of our dating relationship. Five days later, we looked at each other and said, "I think this is *it*." And it was. A friendship was born out of realizing we shared similar interests and hopes and dreams for the future.

Intentionality

It's exciting to know someone else in this gigantic world understands you and can join in your adventure. Think about your best and longest-standing friendship. Maybe you can trace it back as far as childhood when one of you stood up for the other against the playground bully, or you discovered you share an intense love for your hometown bakery's cinnamon rolls. Or maybe your best friend walked into your life in college and invited you to join their sorority or men's softball team when you were homesick and in need of a friend. However the relationship started, the friendship grew and has continued because you have both intentionally nurtured it. Why do we expect our friendship with our spouse to be any different?

Throughout the journey from courtship to the altar, most couples are intentional about the investments we make in the relationship. We prioritize time together, usually at the expense of other responsibilities, friendships, or even sleep! We are driven to know and experience life with each other. Do you remember the feeling?

In his famous book, *The 5 Love Languages*, Dr. Gary Chapman describes this as the "limerence" stage.[2] We are "in love" and compelled to be together. Leaving no stone unturned in our discovery of each other, we inevitably become best friends. The exhilaration we experience during this stage of the relationship leads to a chemical release of dopamine in our brains that keeps us returning to whatever triggered these feelings of euphoria. That connection is called dopamine bonding.

That makes sense when you're dating, but that stage wears off after a few years. What does this mean in marriage? In essence, although it's unlikely we'll return to that same "limerence" we experienced in our new dating relationship, we can intentionally stimulate this reaction when we choose to date our spouse. When you have fun and laugh together, you experience a dopamine hit that creates a positive bond. Every couple I've ever counseled has a deep desire to get back to that feeling of limerence.

Bonnie and I were married for thirteen years before God chose to bless us with our first child. We would hear couples talk about "date night," and it didn't register with us. We did everything together, worked together, played together, dreamed of, and ran a ministry together. All in a twenty-four-foot motorhome, I might add! Why on earth would we need a date night?

Enter sweet baby, Josie. We were so smitten by this little cooing answer to prayer. But heeding the advice of several godly couples, we dropped off that five-day-old bundle of long-awaited joy with some friends and started our dating journey. When Josie was six months old, we re-connected with a couple whose son had played in our student worship band several years before. With both of our parents living a few hours away from us, Rick and Deborah, or "Mr. Wick" and "Deba," as our children called them, were an incredible blessing to our family.

They said that when their children were young, they had an older couple keep their two little ones to allow them to go on weekly date nights, and they promised they would one day pay that ministry forward. We were the recipients of that great gift! They kept Josie, then eventually Colby, three out of four Friday nights a month for us, for several years, until God moved them away. Our children couldn't wait for Friday nights to roll around so they could go spend time with "Mr. Wick" and "Deba." They would wave 'good-bye' to us with big ole smiles on their faces and say the line their "in-town grandparents" had trained them to say, "have fun on your hot date!"

We can't attest to how "hot" all of those dates were. Some nights we went out to dinner or a movie. Others, we went on bike rides or runs. Some nights we finished up house projects or just ordered pizza and crashed on the couch. We may not have done anything fancy, but we were intentional. We talked, laughed, shared our hearts, and dopamine bonded.

The Way of Friendship

Women often complain to me (Bonnie) that their husbands won't talk to them. They desire to have heart talk, but they feel like their man refuses to open up. The thing about it is, men and women tend to experience friendships differently. Haven't you noticed? Women have this natural desire to talk and open up. That's why you will see two women meeting for lunch for so long that the waitress feels like she deserves a double tip for keeping her table tied up. Women want to talk, reflect, connect, and dig into matters of the heart. Women most enjoy relationships face-to-face. There's satisfaction in needing and feeling needed by someone. It speaks to our design.

On the other hand, (Daniel here), men are better at friendships when we can experience them shoulder to shoulder. That's why men typically hang out on a golf course or watch a ballgame or in our workplace. Men talk and might even begin to open up as we share a common interest or work together toward a common mission. Does that sound familiar? Men need a mission. Sometimes we don't talk; we just grunt.

Because we don't feel like our spouse experiences friendship the way we do, too often, we decide it's best to let same-sex relationships outside the marriage meet our friendship needs. While it's important to foster relationships with our guy friends or girlfriends, those relationships shouldn't take precedence over a friendship with our spouse. God saw that man needed a companion, a friend, and He gave him a woman to share life with, not another guy. It stretches men and women to give of themselves to meet each other's friendship needs.

When my (Bonnie's) Mama married my Daddy, he moved her out into the middle of three hundred acres of family farmland and pine trees. He loved to deer and bird hunt, fish, ride horses, and just be outside. Mama quickly adopted the "if you can't beat em, join em" mentality and jumped headlong into Daddy's hobbies. Through the years, they became the very best of friends as they had fun side by side. And you know what else? She became a better shot than Daddy! The trophy buck that stared at us from over the mantle in our living room belonged to Mama. It was displayed there by her very proud husband.

Women, we need to work at doing life side-by-side with our husbands because they need our companionship and for us to show interest in what they are accomplishing. The heart of a man more naturally unfolds when his guard is down during side-to-side interaction. Wife, if you want your husband to open up to you, try engaging in a hobby that he enjoys. Gaming or football may not sound fun, but you never know, you might discover a new hobby!

Likewise, men, wives need for you to meet them in the middle and get better at face-to-face interaction. Women have a deep desire to be known and to have their hearts discovered. That comes through conversation. They want to see that you enjoy them, exclusively. Meaning, no one else gets the same kind of face time with you that they do. Nobody gets the same window and insight into your life that your wife does. Intimate talk doesn't usually come naturally to men, but it holds the key to your wife feeling loved. Isn't it worth taking the time to develop this skill?

As a Dad, I recently struggled to find ways to connect with Josie. Colby is easy, just grab a ball or turn on the game, and he's good. However, even though Josie's personality is most like mine, she doesn't have a hobby that is easy to connect over. I've recently realized what reaches the heart of my daughter is talking! Josie enjoys nothing more than grabbing a milkshake or a cup of coffee at our local "Five Bucks" coffee shop and sitting for an hour and talking. Husbands, if you'll do this with your wife (and daughters), you'll build a strong and deep intimate friendship.

It comes naturally during courtship, but remaining best friends over a lifetime takes work. It's yet another way you can serve each other and allow God to love your spouse through your dependency on Him to fill you with His attributes. Though you have and need other close friends, your best friend should be your spouse. The word "best" implies that you pursue and choose each other over all others. This doesn't mean you can't cultivate same-sex friendships. You need those, too, but intimate friendship with your spouse makes living a life pointed toward a mission a whole lot more enjoyable.

Listen to *The Marriage Adventure Podcast,*
Episodes 4 & 5 to learn more about how important
the friendship factor is in your marriage.
www.themarriageadventure.com/podcasts

Transparency and a Soft Place to Land

One of the things we value most about our longest
and deepest friendships is the ability to be transparent with our friends. I (Bonnie) have had only a few
of what I call "heart friends" throughout my life. God
gifted one of these to me shortly after we moved here
seventeen years ago (at the time of this writing). Kim
and I got to know each other in a couples small group
Bible study that we both attended. God eventually
led us to start meeting together weekly to study the
Bible and encourage and pray for each other.

Kim has been a trusted confidant and prayer war-
rior in my life. She prayed and cried with me through
five years of infertility; then, she rejoiced with me at
the hospital on the day of my daughter's birth. This
dear friend held me up spiritually and even literally
when she drove hours to be with me when my Daddy
died and on the dark days that followed. Kim knows
my heart and loves me anyway. After all, "A friend
loves at all times, and a brother is born for adver-
sity" (Prov. 17:17). I feel safe enough with Kim to be
transparent.

Because we value friendships and seldom want to
lose them, most of us tend to shield our friends from
some of the darkness we allow to be unleashed in our
marriage relationships. Our hearts feel safe with our
"besties," and theirs with us, so we are careful to protect those friendships. So, why doesn't this apply to

our friendship with our spouse? It's vitally important that we value our marriage friendship above even the others we hold so dearly. As close as I am with my friend, I can honestly say, that not even Kim knows me the way Daniel does. The only way we will experience connectivity and transparency in our marriage is to work hard to create a safe haven for each other.

Over time, something beautiful and terrible happens in marriage. We let our guard down enough to become transparent with one another. We can reveal our true selves and let our spouse see all of our shining qualities. This intimacy is a taste of what God desires for us to have with Him. He created us, knows us better than we can ever know ourselves, and He loves us anyway! Christ sees us for who we are in Him, without spot or blemish. Sounds a little like unending limerence doesn't it?

But on the flip side of marital transparency, we let our guard down and unleash the selfish beast that inevitably rears his ugly head. We feel secure enough in our commitment to say things and act ways around the person who lives with us that we would NEVER expose to anyone else. We have got to find ways to diligently pursue this level of transparency with each other without damaging our relationship. We must work to become a refuge for each other. Transparency can only exist in a relationship in which we feel completely safe.

When Josie, our oldest, started kindergarten, I felt led to leave my job as Programming Director at our church and stay home. I wanted to be more available for our children, but it was more than that. Daniel and I had worked side by side in the Worship Ministry for almost twenty years, and with his move into the new role of Executive Pastor, our work dynamic changed. Because of the confidential nature of his relationships with my co-workers, he could no longer openly discuss his workday with me. And because my co-workers answered to Daniel, I no longer felt free to discuss aggravations I had at work. Pillow talk suddenly became inappropriate venting to my boss. For the first time in our marriage, I felt disconnected and like we couldn't be transparent about all aspects of our lives.

Once again, wisdom from Mama impacted my marriage. As I shared my frustration over this new dilemma, and she gave me counsel, one phrase wrapped itself around my heart. She said that no matter what kind of day a man experiences out in the world, he always needs to feel like he can walk through the door of his home and have a soft place to land—Mama's message sunk in. That was a big part of why I felt God tugging on my heart to step away from my job at the church. I had a great desire for our home to be a peaceful environment for my husband and children, but that required me to make space in my overloaded brain and give up even good things to make me a safe haven for Daniel.

This world can be harsh outside the walls of our homes. We're not implying that one of you needs to quit your job and become a stay-at-home-mom or dad. What we are saying is relationally, we need to be the safest person in our spouse's life and create the safest environment possible for each other. This kind of safety is best built through trust. It says, "I can trust you not to hurt me. I can trust you to be all in through the hard times. I can trust you to keep my secrets. I can trust you to believe the best about me. I can trust you to protect me. I can trust you to see through my worst days and love me anyway. I can trust you to fight for me and us." Trust can be incredibly difficult to rebuild once broken, which is why it's so essential to guard it if you have it.

Forgiveness

I recently sat with a couple in my office that had experienced a severing of trust. The husband had confessed his violation of their marriage covenant with another woman but was desperate to repair his marriage. His wounded wife was trying hard to forgive but struggled with lashing out every time they got in an argument. It had been almost a year since the affair. Still, he felt every disagreement or accidental disappointment ripped his wife's wound open. She could throw a reminder of his indiscretion in his face and promptly end any argument.

This response is typical when trust is broken to this degree. All I had to offer the tormented wife was the advice I give other couples; "For the rest of your life, you hold a trump card that will immediately end and win every argument. But your greatest victory and the key to moving through this is choosing never to use it."

Once trust is broken, it damages the integrity of any relationship. When someone doesn't follow through with the small things or repeatedly breaks their word to you, you view them as a little less safe. You become more guarded, pull back, or even sever the relationship to protect your heart. In the marriage covenant, it's not that simple.

The most painful wounds are typically inflicted by the people closest to us. When the breach comes through deep betrayal in the most sacred spaces of your marriage and your trust is severed, is there hope? Absolutely, but it can be a daunting and treacherous uphill climb. Repairing damage in the foundation of trust can only happen when we are willing to extend something supernatural to our spouse called grace.

Creating a soft place for your spouse to land says, "you are safe enough to mess up, and I will still choose to love you." Grace is putting up with each other when we fall short and choosing to forgive the way God forgave us. The Apostle Paul tells us that, as God's chosen, holy, and dearly loved people, we are to clothe ourselves or cover ourselves with compassion, kindness, humility, gentleness, and patience. And the Lord knows, those are all the Christ qualities we need so we can, "Bear with each other and forgive one another if any of you has a grievance against someone. Forgive as the Lord forgave you. And over all these virtues put on love, which binds them all together in perfect unity" (Col. 3:12-14, NIV).

That's pretty tough stuff. Forgive if you have a grievance against someone. That means we offer grace for the little things that invade our personal happiness, but it also means we have to show our spouse grace for the big stuff. Grace chooses to extend forgiveness to our spouse as Jesus forgave us, *completely*. We can only forgive and offer this kind of grace out of an overflow of an abiding relationship with Christ. Only Jesus can empower us to love in a way that "keeps no record of wrongs" (1 Cor. 13:5, NIV).

It's human nature to store past grievances in a little back closet of our hearts and pull them out as weapons when we need them. But the grace God showed us in the forgiveness of our very condition of sin has wiped our record clean. The extent of compassion, kindness, humility, gentleness, and patience that it takes to move through the ongoing process of extending grace and forgiveness in marriage can only come from God allowing us to see our spouse the way Christ sees and loves them.

In his book, *Grace Filled Marriage,* Tim Kimmel explains it this way. "The contradiction for the Christian is to be a willing recipient of the grace God offers us but reluctant to extend the same gift to our spouse. How ironic that the missing ingredient in our marriage when we act that way is the primary ingredient in God's heart when He deals with us."[3]

We recognize that there are circumstances some marriages just cannot overcome. There are other resources offering counsel on this, and we urge you to speak with a Christian counselor or pastor if you have experienced broken trust in your marriage to this degree. But even in the instances of the worst betrayals to the marriage covenant, we have seen God miraculously restore hope and even trust where it seemed impossible.

Lots of couples make a conscious commitment to continue onward in their mission together. But if couples want to remain friends, we must be intentional about having fun together, sharing our hearts, and creating a safe place for transparency and trust in the marriage. Friendship keeps drawing our hearts back to our mission. Our relationship is more solidified by the shared experiences of the challenges and victories that brought us to each milestone along the way. There is something about the thrill of the journey that not only bonds you as friends but leads to something far more exciting... intimate friendship.

Listen to *The Marriage Adventure Podcast, Episodes 53 & 54* to learn more about how vital it is to have a grace filled marriage. www.themarriageadventure.com/podcasts

CHAPTER 11:

FRIENDTIMACY

As day ten of our two-week family adventure was coming to a close, I began to reflect on our trip of a lifetime. Everything had mostly gone as planned. Our kids had enjoyed every minute of it with barely a cross word between them. The long trip out to the Grand Canyon and Sedona, in many ways, was as fun as the destinations. Everything was so fresh, and each day promised a new experience.

Daniel and I couldn't have asked for more from the kids, the motorhome, or the vacation. But, as I reflected on our almost completed mission, I felt a little like something was lacking. We had driven a large section of Route 66, had seen breathtaking views of the Grand Canyon and picturesque scenes everywhere we turned in Sedona. Oh, what fun we had had as a family! But there's one thing you really can't do in a 30-foot motorhome with children sharing the same space. It's *nearly* impossible to connect sexually! Notice the emphasis is on nearly. I'll just leave it at that.

That's one of the many reasons we suggest to couples to take one vacation with your kids, and another one with just your spouse if at all possible! As impressive as it was to see so much of God's beautiful creation, it paled in comparison to experiencing the depths of another person's heart.

Fashioned to Fit

Many times, as I meet with couples in counseling sessions, I'll ask, "When was the last time you had sex or were intimate?" Sadly, the answer typically isn't a good one. When a couple is in a bad place, sex is usually the first thing to go, or it went long ago. That's because sex is an overflow out of an intimate friendship. The good news is that it can remedy itself rather quickly once they can get their friendship back on track.

How does friendship factor into the sexual relationship? Men, you may be interested in the statistic from studies by the Gottman Institute that "the determining factor in whether wives feel satisfied with the sex, romance, and passion in their marriage is, by 70%, the quality of the couple's friendship."[1] When the friendship suffers, the sexual relationship suffers. A thriving friendship between husband and wife lays the foundation for an intimate, satisfying sexual relationship between man and woman.

Living life on a mission together binds you. You get to experience the beauty of your journey together. But friendship is not enough for the long-haul journey of your lifelong Marriage Adventure. Your heart connection should make you long for a physical one. In essence, a healthy sex life is one benefit of moving through life with a common purpose. The other side of that coin is that you won't feel satisfied in a fulfilled mission if you are not experiencing each other intimately. There is a very good reason for that.

There is something mystifying and breathtaking about reading the Creation account in Genesis. "In the beginning, God created the heavens and the earth" (Gen. 1:1). God said, "let there be light," and darkness fled. He commanded the universe into existence. He spoke and the waters rolled back to expose land. The words from His mouth created vegetation on land, the sun, moon, and stars in the heavens, fish in the seas, and birds in the air. He told the earth to bring forth living creatures and it was so. All of God's creation was spoken into existence, except one.

"Then the Lord God formed the man of dust from the ground and breathed into his nostrils the breath of life, and the man became a living being... Then the Lord God made a woman from the rib he had taken out of the man, and he brought her to the man" (Gen. 2:7; 22, NIV).

Did you catch that? God *formed* man, and *made* woman. He fashioned us with His own hands, then breathed His breath into us to bring us to life!

> God made you from one cell from your mom, meeting up with one cell from your dad. Each cell carries 23 chromosomes. The one from your mom was carrying half of her DNA, the one from your dad was carrying half of his DNA, and those two cells met and merged into one single cell, and when they did, those chromosomes matched, and when they did, they began to form, together, a brand-new DNA code... using four characters, four nucleotides... and they began to write out what is the three billion-character description of who you are written in the language of God, describing who God had ordained you to be. If you took the DNA out of that one little cell that made you and stretched it out, that DNA would be six feet long... three billion characters stretched out to six feet long. If a person were to read your DNA one character

per second night and day, it would take that person 96 years to just read your description.[2]

With such incredible attention to every detail of our creation, little is more fascinating than how God intricately formed men and women to fit. He made every part of us on purpose and with purpose. We are different, yet complementary to each other anatomically. Not only do men and women fit together to become one physically during sex, but the two become one emotionally. There is unity. God ensured that the physical act of intercourse would emotionally bond us together by having oxytocin release in our brains' pleasure centers, which creates an addictive response to the physical action. Even science supports the bonding that takes place when a sexual encounter results in orgasm.

> Orgasms aren't just for fun...they contribute to our sense of connection in a relationship. University of California, San Francisco found that Oxytocin is released during orgasm. Oxytocin is nicknamed the "cuddle hormone" or the "connection hormone" because it is the tiny little chemical that makes us feel connected and loyal to someone. So when we orgasm, this bonding hormone is released, spurring researchers to believe that a connection should be made if a partner can make you orgasm.[3]

What we find even more remarkable than the chemical release is the way a man's and woman's physical design mirrors their relational and emotional design. Let us explain. God created women to be relational, emotionally desiring to be known. Much of this concept of a man's and woman's needs in this section is derived from the paired works of John and Stasi Eldridge's books, *Wild at Heart* and *Captivating*.[4] When she feels safe in the marriage relationship, she exposes her heart, offering herself to the man she loves. This process takes time because she wants to know if he believes she's worth it. A wife invites her husband to know her. She offers herself, desiring to be deeply discovered and understood, to draw his heart into hers.

Physically, a woman's body operates much the same way. The female form is artistry and alluring to man. She desires to be viewed as beautiful as she unveils herself. She is sexually aroused when she is pursued, tenderly touched, and explored by her husband. Through this discovery, the wife is brought to a place where she wants to pull her husband inside her. Their foreplay culminates in a filling and meeting of one of the deepest desires and needs of a woman's heart. She feels pursued, fought for, won over, and intimately known.

Man's design is no less miraculous. He has a curiosity and a drive to explore. He wants to show himself strong on behalf of his woman. He longs for adventure, to fight for something, and to know that he has what it takes to be a man. When his wife invites him in, he embarks on a journey to explore her body, which inspires him to rise to the occasion physically, show himself strong on her behalf, and come through for her.

Without a husband's passionate pursuit and desire to discover his wife, their intimate act cannot be consummated. As they come together, their physical needs are met, but even more significantly, a man's and woman's heart longings are satisfied. With such incredible attention to detail, there is no question that God created the sexual and marital relationship to be shared between one man and one woman for life.

Jesus reminded us in Matthew 19:4-6 of God's design for oneness. "Have you not read that he who created them from the beginning made them male and female, and said, 'Therefore, a man shall leave his father and his mother and hold fast to his wife, and the two shall become one flesh?' So they are no longer two but one flesh. What therefore God has joined together, let not man separate." The sexual union serves not only to bring pleasure physically, but it binds us together emotionally. Our bodies are joined, and we become one flesh as we become relationally and emotionally intertwined. This type of sharing requires vulnerability.

There is no place in which we become more vulnerable than in the act of intercourse. Even the word "intercourse" infers the interchange of thoughts and feelings through communication with each other. A woman is attracted to her husband when he is trustworthy, attentive to her needs, and she feels safe sharing her heart and life with him. A man is drawn to his wife when she encourages him to be himself, and he feels no risk when he exposes his heart. This is why it's so important to create safety and transparency within the friendship.

To be "naked and unashamed" as Adam and Eve were initially, means there is nothing to hide. In the marriage relationship, God intends for us to become so open, honest, and vulnerable with each other that trusting each other with our bodies and pleasure in the bedroom is an overflow of the intimacy we've created in the relationship.

The sexual relationship should be an expression of our closeness, not the foundation of it. We should feel the greatest freedom to express ourselves uninhibitedly with our spouse. We get to share the secret of what brings each other pleasure in a way that no one else is allowed to experience with us. This is how we become "one flesh."

Early in our marriage, our sexual relationship wasn't all God intended it to be. As a young bride, I battled chronic urinary tract infections for the first two years. We would be intimate a few times; I would get sick, start on an antibiotic (which created other problems) then I would finish out the month with my monthly "ladies' days." There would only be about one week out of the month that we felt free to be intimate. And to be honest, I didn't look forward to it. I knew that having sex would just lead to getting another infection, more antibiotics, and around and around it went. It wasn't until I saw a urologist who helped me deal with the physical issue that I was emotionally open enough to allow myself to enjoy the process of sex... TWO YEARS into marriage! Even then, it took a bit of work to allow me to respond.

We had our most significant breakthrough in year eight. Yep, year eight! When we got married, we did what any financially broke couple with only "major medical" insurance would do. We wanted to prevent pregnancy, so I went on birth control pills. Those pills did precisely what they were supposed to do. What I didn't understand at the time was, those hormones also prevented me from having the desire for sexual intimacy with my husband that God had designed within my body.

When we began trying to conceive after eight years of marriage, I discovered that God also created women with a sex drive and the same capacity to experience intense pleasure that men have. After the hormones got entirely out of my system, I felt robbed of eight years of a gift that God intended to give me. Up to that point, our friendship was wonderful, but adding desire for and experiencing intimacy with my husband in this way, intensified our friendship and bond.

I had read 1 Corinthians 7 many times. In fact, I kind of glossed over this "married sex" passage thinking it was the permission husbands needed to have frequent relations with their uninterested wives, but, for the first time in our marriage, I received 1 Corinthians 7:3 as a gift to me instead of a command. "The husband should fulfill his wife's sexual *needs*, and the wife should fulfill her husband's needs" (NLT).

Wait one second!! Fulfill his wife's sexual *needs*? Believe it or not, God did create women with sexual needs. If that has not been your experience so far, we encourage you to explore the reason or reasons. There might be a physical problem that could be addressed by a physician. Or there might be something much deeper like emotional issues from past sexual experiences or abuse that you should discuss with a counselor. Either way, God desires for both husbands and wives to experience pleasure and incredible satisfaction through the sexual relationship. Don't ignore a lack of it. We'll discuss this a little later in this chapter.

The Gift of Sex

The most personal physical gift we can give to our spouse is our body. 1 Corinthians 7:4-5 explains it this way: "The wife gives authority over her body to her husband, and the husband gives authority over his body to his wife. Do not deprive each other of sexual relations unless you both agree to refrain from sexual intimacy for a limited time so you can give yourselves more completely to prayer. Afterward, you should come together again so that Satan won't be able to tempt you because of your lack of self-control" (NLT).

Don't miss the first sentence of this passage. It's essential. Read it again. The wife *gives* her body to her husband, and the husband *gives* his body to his wife. Sex is to be freely and willingly given as a gift to each other. Sex is never to be taken by force, EVER. The marriage bed is a place to serve each other, not take from one another. An excellent guideline to follow would be never to do anything that would cause physical harm or emotional humiliation. Clear communication is crucial to understanding how to meet one another's needs in this sacred space. Be sure that your spouse feels loved, served, and safe during your time together in the bedroom. If you aren't one hundred percent sure they are experiencing the same pleasure you are, ask them.

Our scripture passage in 1 Corinthians is also clear that sex is not something to be withheld to manipulate or punish. I am a bit surprised when I hear other women say things like, "If he doesn't shape up, he won't be getting sex this week." Or, "He's fine with me going out with my friends because I make it worth his while when I get home."

These kinds of comments indicate deep-seated selfishness about the sexual relationship and the relationship as a whole. God designed sex to be a mutual submission within a loving, devoted, life-long relationship, where we selflessly serve each other to meet one another's physical and emotional needs. Women, we distort God's design, reverting to our inner "Eve" when we use sex as a means to control our husbands.

At the peak of intercourse, we have to entirely abandon control so that we can experience the intensity of erotic pleasure. That's no less true relationally. We must stop trying to control our husbands if we want to experience the fullness of relational intimacy we so desire. Using sex as a weapon or as a prize damages the trust you have with each other, and robs you of the intimacy you can share through your experience.

How Often?

Since the Bible has a lot to say about the sexual relationship between a husband and wife, people have asked us the question that may be on your mind, "How often should we be having sex?" Well, let's look back at verse 5 of our 1 Corinthians passage. "Do not deprive each other of sexual relations unless you both agree to refrain from sexual intimacy for a limited time" (NLT).

You won't find an exact number of times per week or month that you should be intimate with your spouse, but since it is clear that we are not supposed to deprive each other, we'd say the answer is *a lot!* In fact, it indicates that the only reason to take a break is if you both agree to devote yourselves entirely to prayer. Then, when you finish praying, have more sex.

There are valid reasons for this. First, Paul says we are weak and will be tempted to stray if we aren't staying connected sexually with our spouse. Remember the "little foxes" we discussed earlier? Research also provides evidence that regular intercourse offers the health benefits of increasing cardiovascular health, reduced blood pressure, reduced risk of prostate cancer, and increased immune system function. Due to Oxytocin and endorphins' release, sex also serves as a great way to relieve stress.[5]

Remember dopamine bonding? Oxytocin and endorphins are good for us physically. They bond us to each other relationally because we continue to come back for more of this addictive chemical released when we're intimate with our spouse. The brilliance of this design for sex within marriage is undeniable.

Seasons and Reasons

Frequent intimacy certainly keeps you connected with your spouse, but what if it's been quite a while since the sparks were flying? It's important to understand that both men's and women's sex drives go through peaks and troughs in different life seasons. A nursing mother with toddlers clinging to her all day will desire less physical touch than when the nest is empty. A father working sixty-hour weeks pushing toward a deadline will have less energy and drive for sex than a twenty-three-year-old newlywed. Hormonal changes, high levels of stress, depression, grief, alcohol use, and some medications, along with a host of other issues, can affect sexual desire.

One or both of you, will inevitably walk through a difficult or transitional season that will affect your sexual drive. As you age and experience hormonal change, you will most likely find that your desire is declining. This is entirely normal and no cause for alarm, but it is cause for an honest conversation.

It should be obvious that we can't live in the honeymoon stage of our relationship forever. But what if one or the other of you has no interest in sex and doesn't enjoy it? A wife once confessed to me (Bonnie) that she could go the rest of her life without ever having sex again. She went a step further in admitting she was okay with her husband looking at porn if it meant he could be satisfied without her involvement. If either of you feels this way, it indicates a problem that you need to address. A more in-depth conversation with my friend revealed sexual abuse in a past relationship that she had been ignoring and covering for over twenty years.

Another friend of mine expressed that she didn't enjoy sex but went along with her husband because she felt it was her "wifely duty." After talking with her gynecologist, she discovered physical and hormonal reasons her body wasn't responding during intercourse. She was relieved after figuring out what to do differently, and she now enjoys the physical and emotional connection God intended her to have with her husband.

If you have either an emotional or physical aversion to intercourse, we urge you to investigate why. There may be a simple reason, or there might be deep-seated pain from abuse or a past relationship that you need to work through with a qualified counselor. Don't continue to ignore a lack of desire for intimacy with your spouse. We are not saying this road will be easy. It will require vulnerability and honesty, but God wants to bring healing and for you to experience sex as the gift He created it to be.

As you walk through difficult seasons and uncover genuine reasons for lack of sexual intimacy, make sure you face them together. If intimacy is interrupted, you can lean into the close friendship you have nurtured. Be sensitive to the needs of your spouse and transparent about your changing desires. This calls for patience with each other and with yourself. As uncomfortable as the subject may be, it's essential to keep communication lines open to ensure that you move through it together and don't get bogged down in it. Your lack of desire or changing interest will be apparent to your spouse. They may need reassurance that it's a physical or emotional issue and not your attraction to them. Frequency is not nearly as crucial as a continued emotional connection.

Difficult seasons may disrupt intimacy, but nothing influences our passion like the emotional connection we have with our spouse. Showing affection doesn't have to be sexual. Cuddling, hugging, hand-holding, and kissing don't have to culminate in sex but are all important ways to experience intimacy. Physical touch of any kind still releases those feel-good, bonding chemicals that can help you stay close until you can work through a challenging season.

If you find that there is no physical or emotional problem, but things have cooled a little in the bedroom, one of the best ways to rekindle the fire is to be intentional about enjoying each other as friends. You may need to set aside a week or weekend to get away together to have fun. We try to slip away from the kids for one or two weekends every year. We spend that time unwinding, having fun, and enjoying each other. Even though sexual intimacy isn't the foundation of a healthy marriage, it certainly is part of God's design for husbands and wives to keep them emotionally connected.

It's Not About Me

Have you ever been on a team or worked on a project with a "glory hog?" You know the type. Everyone collaborates with brilliant ideas and puts in long hours to prepare for "game day." Then, as your boss takes a seat at the table, "Sam Showoff" proudly takes credit for the team's collective million-dollar idea and gets promoted to the corner office with a view. The whole team may get a "win" or pull off an excellent presentation a few times, but you will begin to resent a selfish teammate over time.

Let's just get this out of the way. There is no place for selfishness in the bedroom! If only one of you regularly experiences satisfaction, there will eventually be a breakdown in this two-person "team sport." It won't be easy to stay on your life's mission if one or both of you don't feel physically connected in your relationship.

We're sure by now you've seen a common thread throughout this book. God has called us to serve our spouse lovingly. We've said before that we should set aside our desire for our spouse to meet our needs and look for ways to allow Christ to love them through us. So, you won't be surprised when we say that we have a fantastic opportunity to serve each other in the bedroom. One of your short-term missions should be for both of you to enjoy your sexual relationship.

As with anything else in life, the enemy plans to take something extraordinary in the sexual relationship and turn it into something self-serving. Whether it's an attitude of *I don't like sex* or *I need to get my needs met,* Satan's plan is to make it all about us; to make us a sexual "glory hog." That's why pornography is so dangerous. Not only is it an industry that is destroying the fabric of our society, but it's also destroying marriages. It is designed for quick, addictive self-gratification. It robs marriages of intimacy and creates an evil fantasy world in the mind of the addicted individual.

Let us go ahead and address the elephant in the room. There is a really strong chance that one of you struggles with pornography, so address the elephant in the room and do all you can to guard your home and personal devices. We recommend husbands and wives be transparent and talk about it. Your most effective form of accountability when it comes to pornography is your spouse. Bonnie has committed to partner with me in this fight. We have filters on all of our devices, and Bonnie holds the passwords. I have nothing to hide; she can see every site I've visited. She also asks me difficult questions. Along with a healthy sexual relationship, this has freed me from any temptation or addiction pornography tries to have over me. God is clear that the only legitimate and holy way to have our sexual needs met is within the boundaries of an intimate, loving marriage relationship with your spouse. Seeking to meet your own sexual desires or not seeking to meet your spouse's, breaks trust that is not easy to rebuild.

So, how do we serve each other in the bed-room? As stated above, when we use sex as a tool of manipulation to get our way, that's selfish and not servant-minded.

A significant step in serving our spouse in the bedroom is to change our mindset about sex from *it's about me* to *it's about my spouse.* If we have the attitude that our goal is to please the other person, ultimately, it will change our experience. Men, this is especially true for us. If we re-orient our thinking and make the entire experience about our wife, we'll ulti-mately have an experience far better than we could ever imagine.

Another way we serve each other is by SLOWING DOWN! Guys, what's your hurry? If your wife does not enjoy sex, you might want to investigate the reason. Are you taking the time to allow her body to respond? A woman's average time to orgasm is substantially longer than a man's; therefore, men, we must take our time. Let your bride know that this is all about pleasing her. Don't get me wrong, a "quickie" is great every once in a while, but learn her cues. There's an old song by the Pointer Sisters that says it all:

I want a man with a slow hand
I want a lover with an easy touch
I want somebody who will spend some time
Not come and go in a heated rush
I want somebody who will understand
When it comes to love, I want a slow hand.

One more way we should serve each other sexu-ally is by understanding the pleasure spots. God cre-ated men and women with "buttons." Learn where those "buttons" are and how and when to push them.

The male and female bodies have about seven erogenous zones. We must serve each other by learning where these zones are and learn how to use them best to bring pleasure to your spouse. Scripture tells us to "study to show ourselves approved" (2 Timothy 2:15, KJV). Okay, so that's taken out of context, but I think that the same advice applies here, too!

Study your spouse. Once you have identified their erogenous zones, find out what your spouse enjoys and is comfortable with, which can be done in two ways. First, you can simply ask them. It may be an uncomfortable question, but if you pick the right time and right environment (probably not in the middle of sex) to ask, it will let them know that your heart is to serve them. The second way to find out what they enjoy is to pay close attention to their verbal and nonverbal cues during sex and keep a mental log.

Men, I like to say that foreplay starts in the morning. It doesn't take much for a man to want to have sex. However, women are a little more complicated creatures. We must make sure that we serve our wife throughout the day by partnering with her to keep the family, kids, and house in order. Taking responsibility and engaging with her is vital.

I never look sexier to Bonnie around my house than when I'm cleaning the bathroom or getting the kids ready for bed. It's basically considered a form of foreplay! No woman wants to have sex with a man who acts like a twelve-year-old. Video games and fantasy football aren't sexy if you are wrapped up in them while she is stepping over you to take care of the home and kids. The childish husband was the entire primus of the TV show *Everybody Loves Raymond*. It's funny on television, but not in real life. I'm not saying that you can't have these things as hobbies, but make sure you keep them in proper balance.

Falling into the rut of doing the same thing, the same way every time, can hijack your sexual relationship. We can serve each other in the bedroom by mixing things up a bit. Get out of your routine and be willing to try new things you are both comfortable with. We want to clarify here that it's never okay to bring other people into your relationship. Hebrews 13:4 sets boundaries, "Honor marriage, and guard the sacredness of sexual intimacy between wife and husband. God draws a firm line against casual and illicit sex" (MSG). But the marriage bed is a place you should be able to freely express yourselves and enjoy each other like no other. No one else in the world gets to experience you in this way.

Another way to keep it fresh is by swapping up the planning. Yes, that's right, we said planning. It may not sound romantic, but scheduling and planning sex is a great way to take the guesswork out of it. If something is important to you, you typically make an appointment and keep it. When you are in a busy season of life, you may have to send your spouse an "event" invitation to add "quickie" to their calendar. But getting an invitation in the middle of the day from your spouse sure can give you something to look forward to and begin building anticipation. It also keeps intimacy a priority and allows time for "planned spontaneity."

Swapping up the planning means you equally take responsibility for initiating and planning your time together. Taking turns takes the pressure off of one person and makes it more fun. Ladies, don't leave it entirely up to your husband to spice up your love life. God gave you more than one room in your house, so use them! Every once in a while, grab your husband and pull him into a room for a quick surprise. We're pretty sure he will appreciate the gesture.

Over time, boredom can set in and be an intimacy killer. You don't want to view sex as something to check off your list. But you also don't want to neglect to make time for each other and pursue ways to keep affection and romance an active part of your adventure!

One Flesh

When God created men and women, He could have chosen any design. He could have allowed human multiplication to be clinical, functional, merely a physical process to fertilize an egg with sperm, but in His extraordinary love for us, our grand Creator made it something more. He made the sharing of bodies to be emotional, exciting, and pleasurable. God fashioned husbands and wives with the capacity to know and experience each other completely. Intercourse, mentally, emotionally, and physically unites us to our spouse. This is the process of becoming "one flesh." No other human relationship works this way.

The sexual relationship is not merely a way to fulfill a biological urge. It's the natural culmination of a deep friendship between a husband and wife. Our intimate friendship unifies our hearts, resulting in better teamwork, which helps us fulfill our mission. Do you see how these components are intertwined? God designed us to walk in fellowship with Him to be empowered to love, serve, and enjoy our spouse. This kind of marriage won't go unnoticed. Your love for each other will spill over onto your children, then your friends and family, your co-workers, community, and will eventually reflect Jesus to the world. Mission accomplished!

Listen to *The Marriage Adventure Podcast, Episodes 37, 38, & 39* to learn more about how to have a healthy sexual relationship with your spouse. www.themarriageadventure. com/podcasts

CHAPTER 12:

DETOURS AND WIND TURBINES

F eeling a bit overwhelmed, Bonnie and I sat scratching our heads, staring at the mound of gifts piled high on the table, spilling into the booth seats of the RV and onto the floor. We had carefully moved them from a storage bay underneath the coach while the kids slept inches away from us on Christmas Eve.

So far, our trek was exceeding expectations, and our plans had unfolded perfectly! We wanted to arrive at the Grand Canyon on Christmas Eve. It would be perfect; the kids could wake up Christmas morning to an RV filled with Christmas presents at one of the Seven Natural Wonders of the World, and we did. However, it played out slightly differently than in our heads.

What seemed like a few presents under our tree at home looked like a few thousand in our RV! The kids literally wouldn't be able to get out of their beds. While it was inconvenient, it was pretty hilarious.

The next thing we hadn't accounted for was the temperature. We knew it would be cold, but when we woke up on Christmas morning, it was 18 degrees outside. If you paid attention in science class, you know what that means. In a motorhome connected by a hose to an exposed faucet, it means no water. Oh, there was plenty of ice, but not water! *No problem, we'll be fine*, I told myself. "Let's go take a tour of the canyon!"

As I picked up my phone to call to schedule a tour, I suddenly realized this wonder of the world didn't have the wonder of cell phone coverage! *No problem*, I thought. We walked to the front of the campground and caught a shuttle over to the main lodge, thinking we could get more information and schedule a tour there. Nope. It had never crossed our minds that National Park employees celebrate Christmas at home with their families! Argh!!

What I didn't understand in my aggravation was that frozen pipes would trump cell phone coverage in getting us the Grand Canyon tour of a lifetime. When we arrived at the main lodge, I asked if a maintenance worker could stop by our campsite and unthaw the frozen pipe. "Of course," the guy behind the counter said.

As expected, a maintenance worker showed up at our site ready to help. While he was aiming his flame thrower at a frozen spigot, I asked, "We have one day left here at the canyon; what do we need to do?"

He said, "My favorite place is Shoshone Trail." He then proceeded to give me directions to a trail that wasn't on any map. He said something like, "Turn left at a fallen tree, then you'll see a dog, go another mile, and turn right at an old Pepsi sign, 'yadda, yadda, yadda.'"

We wrote down the directions exactly like he said them (minus the chewing tobacco). Believe it or not, we found it. We exited the Hoover Mover and proceeded to hike about 20 minutes on this trail, passing only one or two others along the way. With no trail markers to guide us, we began to question the well-meaning maintenance man's advice.

But when we came to the end of the trail, we had never been so thankful for frozen pipes. What we saw couldn't be seen on any guided tour. It was breath-taking! We walked out on a jagged point and sat for what seemed like hours staring at the Colorado River below and the vast canyon that stretched for miles in front of us.

Off the Beaten Path

Have you ever noticed that few expeditions go exactly as planned? The same is true with the mission for our marriage. We can write our mission statement, see a vision for the future, begin laying our plans, then, WHAM! Something goes wrong, and we end up on a massive detour. Marriage is one of those adventures you can dream of and plan for, but certainly won't follow your charted course.

Don't get discouraged if you think you know where you are going, then hit a few bumps along the way. It's great to plan for the future and dream of a life that influences everyone around you. But what happens when your GPS loses signal, and you take an unexpected detour?

At the beginning of our courtship, we talked for hours about our families, our faith, and the dreams God had written on each of our hearts. It was almost uncomfortable to feel so instantly connected when we barely knew each other. The desires for family and ministry were oddly intertwined like we were writing each other into our own stories. I recall thinking that Daniel was everything I had spent my teenage years praying for in a husband.

When we began our marriage adventure in 1996, we had an incomplete picture of what we were pledging to each other. "For better or for worse, for richer or for poorer, in sickness and health..." Dreams were dreamed of wedded bliss, as life was an open road before us. Our vision for the future included the perfect job, a white house with the picket fence, an obedient Labrador retriever wagging his tail at the door, and eventually a canvas hanging over our mantle of a beautiful family of four. Like most couples, we made promises to each other at the altar with the "for better" days in mind.

We hit a few bumps and potholes along the way, but eight years into our journey, we took an unexpected detour. We shared with you about how God brought our son, Colby, into our family. But we might not have adopted Colby if we hadn't first traveled the lonely, winding, bumpy road of infertility.

For the first eight years of marriage, we traveled from church to church, leading worship for student camps and events. We were incredibly happy with our life on the road. We often wondered if we would ever be moved to disrupt the fun and fruitfulness of our ministry by having children. God had other plans and began to burn the desire on our hearts to add to our family.

At ages twenty-nine and thirty-one, we felt like it might be time to add to our two-some. But why would we doubt that we wouldn't conceive right away? After all, God had finally turned our hearts, and we were ready to go! After a year and a half of trying to become pregnant, we sought medical help and began our journey through infertility.

It significantly stressed our relationship to manage medications, appointments, and intercourse on an unromantic schedule. Because we had chosen to travel this road alone, we withdrew emotionally from some of our friends and family, which took an emotional toll. Nobody knew of our desire to have children, so they just assumed we didn't want them. We endured many comments about us not having or liking children, all-the-while looking at a negative pregnancy test every 28 to 32 days. We were genuinely happy for people close to us who were adding to their own families, but with each new baby came three fresh wounds.

While waiting to become parents, we heard thirty-six pregnancy announcements, attended thirty-six baby showers, and delivered thirty-six post-delivery meals. Yes, as sad as it sounds, we kept count. We identified with Proverbs 30:15, "Three things that are never satisfied, four that never say, Enough! The grave, the barren womb, land, which is never satisfied with water, and fire, which never says, enough" (NIV)! Our empty arms were never satisfied.

It's hard to describe the peaks and troughs we walked through during that season of our marriage. Unfulfilled longing does something to a couple. It either breaks them, driving a wedge of blame between them, or it binds their hearts together in their unified pursuit. It certainly tested our friendship and intimacy, but we chose to lean in rather than pull away from each other. It seemed we took turns being devastated and determined, heartbroken, and hopeful. We mourned together and learned to give each other space and the grace to grieve the way we needed to individually, thereby drawing strength from our shared sorrow.

Four years into the process, in May of 2008, we'll never forget what we can only describe as our "Gethsemane moment." On the night before He was to be handed over for His trial and eventual crucifixion, Jesus went to the garden of Gethsemane to pray. He knew the hard path that lay before Him and begged His Father to find another way to save those He was sent for. Jesus surrendered His own desire praying, "Father, if you are willing, remove this cup from me. Nevertheless, not my will, but yours, be done" (Luke 22:42). In Jesus' "Gethsemane moment," though He didn't like it, He submitted to His Father's plan.

After years of fertility drugs, seven failed inseminations, and two different specialists telling us our chances were diminishing instead of increasing each month, we relented. Our fervent prayers asking God to change our situation simultaneously began to change. They went from, "Dear God, please fix this and give us a baby!" to "We don't understand it, but we want your way more than our own."

That's when we stopped. We didn't stop praying and crying out to God. But we stopped taking fertility medicine, stopped going to doctors, and stopped charting and planning sex based on ovulation. We just needed to take a break from the stress of trying to add to our family and instead invest our time in comforting and loving each other. We learned to adjust our expectations. This was, by no means, part of the vision we had laid out for our marriage adventure, but, rather than become angry and bitter at God and each other for our unfulfilled expectations, we began to express it as a healthy desire and sought God's direction for remapping our mission.

Over the next three months, our hearts began to heal as we individually and corporately worshiped. We remembered what it was like to simply love each other while serving and ministering to other people. Our bitterness had been broken up and replaced with joy as we started discussing the possibility of adoption. But something happened at the end of August that renewed our desire to conceive.

At my annual gynecological checkup, my doctor finally found something that might be the cause of our infertility. So, we scheduled surgery for October 31st, 2008. That procedure finally provided answers and resolutions to our questions. Per doctors' recommendation, we planned to give my body time to rest and heal at least until the New Year before getting serious about pregnancy again. There's a funny thing about plans. We can make them, but God in His sovereignty is the only one who can fulfill or thwart them. "The heart of man plans his way, but the Lord establishes his steps" (Prov. 16:9).

Two months later, God had a surprise for us. On Christmas morning, without the help of physicians, medications, calendaring, or intentionality, after 60 or more "minus' signs, we saw the first "plus" sign on a pregnancy test! After almost five years of disappointment, we were actually surprised to find out God had created a new life in my womb.

On August 26th, 2009, our first little miracle, Josie Weatherly Hoover, made her appearance. Almost two years later, we adopted our son, Colby Daniel Hoover. On this side of infertility, thirteen years later, the emotions are still fresh. Tears well up out of nowhere as we recall and retell what felt like a five-year detour through the desert. Even as we rejoice in knowing God fulfilled our deepest desire, the pain of the process resurfaces without warning. We didn't ask to travel that particular road filled with disappointment after disappointment. But on this side of it, knowing what we know now, we wouldn't go back and rewrite our story. We are both changed because of the unmarked path God led us down to move us toward His plans.

We learned to love and trust each other and our heavenly Father completely differently through the path of infertility. We kept holding each other up along the way. Even more importantly, we never stopped crying out to God to come through for us. We found that He was big enough to handle our hurt and anger toward Him. But we also found that through all of our kicking and screaming, our Savior was loving enough to wrap his arms around us and draw us closer as He reshaped us. And He was kind enough to stand His ground to give us what we most needed instead of what we thought we wanted.

Listen to *The Marriage Adventure Podcast, Episode 28* to hear our journey through infertility and what God taught us. www.themarriageadventure.com/podcasts

Were we happy about five years of infertility? Absolutely not. The mission we had mapped for adding to our family was a straight shot with few twists and turns. Our motive was pure, but God's chosen route looked different. We eventually both reached a point of desperation that led us to throw up our hands in surrender to whatever path God had for us, with or without children.

Through our detour, we experienced what it was like to find sufficiency in Christ instead of in our weary partner. Neither of us was strong enough to carry the weight of infertility for the other. It was unfair for us to expect each other to be what only Christ could be for us.

Oh, how thankful we are that God didn't answer the prayers we were praying for those five years! Our children that we adore and wouldn't trade for any other in the world wouldn't be our children. We wouldn't be the same parents or have the same marriage relationship. God used that detour to teach us things we wouldn't have learned in any other way.

Don't be discouraged when your vision and mission are not completed in the way or in the timing you expected. Sometimes God takes us on unwanted detours to align our lives with the plan He has had for us all along. We had plans for our journey and were frustrated when we couldn't stay on our planned course, but if God had not delayed our journey, we wouldn't be on mission today. You never know when an unexpected detour is going to lead to the most incredible view of your adventure.

Harnessing the Wind

It felt like I was wrestling a bear as I struggled to keep from being blown off the road when a semi passed us on the left. The wind had picked up along the flat stretch of highway, and my knuckles were starting to turn white on the steering wheel. Daniel had driven through familiar terrain through Georgia, Alabama, Mississippi, Tennessee, and Arkansas, all in day one, so it was only fair for me to give him a break 800 miles into our trek.

Day two held a little more excitement as the scenery out the windows began to flatten, and the trees became sparser. Somewhere along Interstate-40 that ran parallel to old Route 66 in "nowhere, Oklahoma," I started seeing something that made sense of the wind gusts that made it challenging to keep our home on wheels in a single lane. Off in the distance, miles and miles of giant towers with turning arms were clumped together across the countryside. Call me crazy, but I was fascinated by the gargantuan wind turbine farms that followed us from Oklahoma through Texas.

After Daniel took the wheel to finish driving the last leg that day, I started looking up information about wind turbines. I'm not one to dig into the mechanics of electricity, but this concept intrigued me. It's pretty simple, actually. Instead of using electricity to make wind like a fan, wind turbines bridle the wind to produce electricity. While our motorhome fought against the power of the wind, these robot-looking giants harnessed it!

When God has written a mission on our hearts for something grand and adventurous, it's natural to go after it with gusto. You and your spouse can be entirely on the same page with your short-term and long-term goals and even be making progress, but if you are only fueled by your own vision, passion, and determination, you will eventually lose focus, and your mission will fizzle.

If God has given a direction for your lives, He will provide the resources and spiritual strength to reach the intended finish line. Far too often, we set out with God's road map but turn off our GPS and forge the way alone. We can allow ourselves to drive against God's plans, determined to do things our way, in our strength, or we can be filled with the Holy Spirit and allow Him to fuel our mission.

Remember the couple in Eden? When God first commissioned Adam and Eve, they were walking and talking with Him. They lived in fellowship with God and allowed Him to direct their path. At some point, after accepting the mission God had given, they decided to step out and accomplish it independent of His power.

We hope your journey to dependence on God is far less dramatic than ours. But be prepared that God will do whatever it takes to bring you to a place of letting Him take control of your life. If you find your identity in anything or anyone besides Him, you won't have the strength to fulfill His purpose for your life and marriage. The good news is He wants you to be empty of "self" so He can fill you with His power. That's the only sure way to stay on mission.

Dependent Living

It doesn't feel natural to sit in the passenger seat. As the man of the family, I much prefer to drive. After all, the driver is in control of where everyone else is going. Riding in the back seat requires too much dependence on someone else to keep us safe and get us where we are going. That's why it was tough to let Bonnie take the wheel and give me a break from driving.

When we have spent a lifetime of relying on ourselves for where we are going and what we are doing, dependence on God doesn't feel natural either. But if we are going to accomplish the mission God has given us as a married couple, we must learn to move from independent living to dependency on Christ.

Jesus provided the ultimate example of dependency on God. In John 13, we see Jesus at the Feast of the Passover, on the night before His death. In this story, Jesus knew the hour had come that He would leave this world and go back to the Father. He fully understood that He was on the most extraordinary rescue mission of all time under the authority of Almighty God. All of fallen humanity would be brought back into an eternal relationship with a Holy God if Jesus could remain on mission. Only dependency on His Heavenly Father would give Jesus the power to accomplish the daunting task at hand. So, how did He do it?

The first thing we see is that Jesus had security in the relationship with His Father. Being secure in this relationship gave Jesus a clear picture of who He was and confidence in His unpopular mission. Not only was He blessed, loved, and on a mission from His Father, He also had been given authority over everyone and everything on Earth. As Son of the Almighty God, His power and authority were unmatched. He had the upper hand in all situations. That's what made His first action so astonishing.

In this passage, we see that Jesus took off His outer garments and laid them aside. He uncovered Himself, laid himself bare, becoming completely exposed and vulnerable before His disciples. What a risky move! He set aside His right to be right or in charge or to have the upper hand. He humbled Himself.

Next, He grabbed a towel and began to wash the disciples' feet. The disciples had followed Jesus all this time and understood His authority. He was the One who should be exalted and served, so it astonished them when their leader placed Himself at their feet. They never expected this. Jesus not only served them, but He lowered Himself to a place where He had to deal with all the filth they had picked up from their travels through the world that day. He wasn't too proud to get down in the muck of their mess and clean them up.

In John 13:15, Jesus outright tells His disciples, "For I have given you an example, that you also should do just as I have done to you." Jesus has called every one of us to follow His example, to lower ourselves, even when we are justified not to. He calls us to remove the outer garments of pride we may have been hiding behind and become vulnerable enough to willingly expose ourselves to whatever wounds may be inflicted on us in the process. Ouch!

It may feel counterintuitive, but only the assurance of your calling and connection with Christ will empower you to fulfill your mission humbly. This path of service doesn't feel glorious, but it's the path of dependence on God. As we move toward our marriage mission, Jesus calls us to serve our spouse the way He did His disciples.

We know what you must be thinking right now. *If I serve my spouse that way, if I give up the upper hand, lay down my right to be right, expose my heart, making myself vulnerable, and simply serve, how do I get my needs met? Won't my spouse take advantage of me?* That's a great question. Here's the hard answer in a nutshell. Possibly. Jesus washed the feet of every disciple in the upper room that night, and you know what happened? One of them betrayed Him with a kiss of death, setting in motion his journey to the cross. Another one denied Him three times, and only one was present when He died.

We can't tell you that becoming vulnerable enough to serve your spouse, family, and those around you won't lead to your own cross. But, we can tell you that when we are led to a cross through obedience to the Father, He usually has plans to deal with our sins once we get there. We can also tell you that on the other side of that death to self is an experience far better than the façade we were hiding behind before. It's called abundant life. Through that life, we are set free to love as Jesus loved. It's there that we finally encounter selfless, agape love. John tells us that, "This is how we know what love is: Jesus Christ laid down his life for us. And we ought to lay down our lives for our brothers and sisters" (1 John 3:16, NIV).

How does Christ meet my needs? If I allow Him to fill me by spending time in His word, thinking about Him, praying to Him, and seeking His direction for my life, then moment-by-moment, over time, He will begin to transform me from the inside out. This is what fellowship with Christ is all about. Remember Jesus' understanding of His relationship with the Father? His security and identity came from the Father, not from people, which freed Him to serve. He didn't have to have His needs met by the disciples or anyone else. His relationship with His Father was enough. He could make Himself completely vulnerable and serve others, knowing his Father would ultimately put all things right in His life.

Here's a question to ponder. What if God has called me into a relationship with Himself so that I can experience His love through a relationship dependent solely on Him, then allow myself to become the primary conduit of that love to my spouse? Let's repeat that question. What if God has called me into a relationship with Himself so that I can experience His love through a relationship dependent solely on Him, then allow myself to become the primary conduit of that love to my spouse?

Christ wants to reproduce His life through me so that my spouse and everyone in my inner circle will experience His love. I'm not dependent on my spouse to make me happy. My primary function is to serve my spouse and let the Lord pour Himself into me. As He pours into me, I then pour Him out to my family. There is so much He wants to give to your spouse, and He wants to use you as a primary delivery method.

Not too long ago, the forecast was calling for about a week of heavy rain. I (Daniel) began to think *I need to clean out my gutters*. You can tell you're older than forty when you are thinking about your gutters! I grabbed the ladder and climbed up to find that I was right. The gutters on my house were full of leaves, so I spent a few hours cleaning them. When the rain finally came, the water flowed nicely. What is the job of gutters? Their purpose is to move the rainwater in a particular direction, away from the foundation of your house. God purchased you and wants to use you to move His love in a specific direction, toward your spouse, then to your children, then out to the rest of the world.

When we spend our time expecting our spouse to meet our needs, our focus is still on managing our facade, not being a gutter or a conduit of His love. It's more about getting our needs met than serving to meet theirs and show them real love, Christ's love. So, if I'm God's intended vessel to funnel His love to my spouse, then I have to shift my thought process about what I want to get *from* my spouse and ask God to show me what I need to give *to* my spouse. My marriage's primary purpose now becomes loving my spouse well, even when they aren't loving, even when they aren't serving me. I love unconditionally. If you are reading this and thinking, *I don't have the strength to love my spouse like this; then* you are absolutely right! That's why it's so important to walk with Christ.

When it comes to finding the energy to carry out our marriage mission, it's a good idea to use the wind turbine principle. If we can stay connected to Jesus, the One who has called us to our mission, He will supply all the natural energy we need to keep moving forward. Jesus is far better at loving others and living this life than we are. If we let Him work through us and renew us every day, we will keep powered up and fueled for this great marriage adventure. That is truly the only way we will have the energy to keep pouring out and serving our spouse while working toward our mission.

CHAPTER 13:

MISSION DRIFT

When you read blog posts and watch vlogger videos about Sedona, they make it look easy. In reality, you won't find clear markers for some of these unique rock formations on the side of the road. Many aren't marked at all! That's why I feared we would miss something spectacular.

One of the rare gems we wanted to find was a secret cave at the end of Soldier Pass Trail. The problem with this trail is that there are so many cool things to see along the way you kind of forget why you got on the trail in the first place. Soldier Pass Trail is a 4.7 mile heavily trafficked loop trail. The scenery is incredible. First, you pass a cool sink-hole called Devil's Kitchen. A quarter-mile later, you come to one of Sedona's most visited sites, The 7 Sacred Pools. The Apache and Yavapai tribes considered these pools sacred because they held drinkable water year-round, attracted wildlife, and symbolized life and fertility in an otherwise harsh environment. They are really cool! See, you've already forgotten about the cave, haven't you? After we saw the pools, I asked Bonnie, "Are you sure you still want to find this cave? I'm tired."

She said, "Isn't that why we came on this trial?"

"Oh yeah, I forgot," I said. After stopping and asking several times if this was the correct path, we finally came to the cave. I am so glad we pressed on. The cave was remarkable. The nine-year-old boy in me reared his adventurous head as we climbed up into the second level of Batman's secret lair!

Off by One Degree

I think the pursuit of adventure has always been in my blood. I got it honestly. You see, my Grandfather was an Eagle Scout. Then my Dad became an Eagle Scout, and my three older brothers followed in his footsteps. Then, at age sixteen, I earned my Eagle. We all started at the same place, earning the Boy Scout rank, and then worked our way up to Eagle. We did this by earning merit badges that showed proficiency in different skills. One of the badges I had to achieve was for Orienteering. That's a big word for a little kid, but it meant I had to learn how to use a compass and maps to find my way.

We didn't have GPS back then, so I won't elaborate on how many times I got lost in the woods. I will tell you that I know where you can end up when you don't follow the compass exactly. What happens when you are off by one single degree? You may not notice it immediately. After 100 yards, you'll only be off by 5.2 feet. A mile later, you'll be off by 92.2 feet. That doesn't seem like a big deal. But if you continue off course by one degree, after traveling all the way around the earth, you'd miss your destination by 435 miles!

You see, the enemy doesn't have to completely wreck our marriage to keep us from being a beacon of light for Jesus. He simply has to keep us off track by one degree. We can even have a good marriage and not fulfill God's best plan for our lives. Satan knows that if he can keep us distracted by good things, we will drift off course, forfeiting the best.

Living on mission requires us to fix our eyes on Jesus and run the race before us. The writer of Hebrews implores us to stay on course.

> Therefore, since we are surrounded by such a great cloud of witnesses, let us throw off everything that hinders and the sin that so easily entangles. And let us run with perseverance the race marked out for us, fixing our eyes on Jesus, the pioneer and perfecter of faith. For the joy set before him he endured the cross, scorning its shame, and sat down at the right hand of the throne of God. Consider him who endured such opposition from sinners, so that you will not grow weary and lose heart (Heb. 12:1-2, NIV).

If our eyes are on Jesus, we'll run the race with endurance. Jesus kept His eye on the joy or the prize of redeeming His bride, and in the end, the cross was worth it. The enemy wants us to get tangled up in our selfishness and the blame game, which prevents us from loving each other well and doing what God has called us to do together. We don't have time to nit-pick each other and quarrel over whose turn it is to unload the dishwasher. Such distractions keep us living off by one degree and make us ineffective in the Kingdom. Jesus is our compass. We have to keep our eyes fixed on Him and course-correct when necessary to keep us moving in the same direction to ensure we reach the destination we desire.

Drifting

A few years ago, Bonnie and I went on a trip for our twentieth anniversary. It wasn't anything fancy. It was quite the opposite. We took the little pull-behind camper we had at the time down to Saint George Island, FL. If you have children, you probably understand that it didn't matter where we went, as long as it was just the two of us. One day, we were looking for something fun to do and noticed an ad for a guided kayak trip.

Believe it or not, kayaking was something we had never done, so we signed up. From the moment we climbed into those kayaks and set out on the water, we were in love! It was both relaxing, adventurous, and kind of a workout. The only problem was, we were on a group tour. We were dying to break off on our own and explore, but they would have frowned on that, mainly since they weren't our kayaks! That little adventure was the beginning of our love of kayaking and paddle boarding. Before we even got home from the trip, we had already purchased two tandem (2-person) kayaks.

The following year for our anniversary, we went back to the ocean, this time with our own kayaks. Keep in mind; we don't live near a beach, but we do live in a town with a nice-sized lake. So, typically when we kayak or paddle board, it's on smooth waters. It's pretty laid back and mostly easy paddling. However, on this trip, we took our tandem kayak out on an ocean waterway.

We set out across the channel to a beautiful and private little island. The conditions were quite different from what we were used to in our lovely quiet lake back home. The wind was smashing our faces, and the waves tossed our little banana boat all around. I remembered the story of Jonah and the whale. I offered to throw Bonnie overboard, and maybe God would make the wind stop, but she didn't see the humor in my comment. Instead, we both paddled as hard as we could. Even short breaks cost us hard-earned ground because the wind and waves would blow us backward and off course.

With our eyes fixed on the little island we were trying to reach; it took every bit of strength we had to continue digging our oars in the water to keep us on course. When we finally got to the other side, we were utterly exhausted. But it was worth it when we were able to spend the day relaxing together on the serene shoreline, marveling at our monumental accomplishment.

Moving toward intentional living may not require you to make earth-shattering alterations in your marriage. It may merely mean re-aligning your attitudes, motives, and purpose for the things you are already involved in. It's living with an awareness of your "why" and intentionally seeking to love the people around you in a way that helps them see their greater purpose, a relationship with Christ.

Returning to the mainland in our kayaks was a breeze with the wind at our backs; it practically carried us to the dock with minimal effort. In your marriage, if you aren't paddling toward a mission, you will most likely move with the current of everyone around you. It's easy to go with the flow and let society dictate where you end up. So, what happens when one day we look up, and we've gotten off track from the common mission God has given us? We aren't locking arms together with our spouse anymore and charging towards the vision of that preferred future. Things aren't bad, but we are no longer paddling with the same energy. What's happening is called mission drift.

Mission drift is one of the subtle ways the enemy tries to derail our marriages, or at least our influence. In their book, *Mission Drift*, Peter Greer and Chris Horst address this issue in organizations, but the same is true in our families. "Without careful attention, you will inevitably drift from your founding mission. It's that simple. It will happen. Slowly, silently, and with little fanfare, organizations routinely drift from their original purpose, and most will never return to their original intent."[1]

Have you ever taken a dip in the ocean? You get in the water to go for a swim or to splash around and jump the waves. A few minutes later, you look back to the beach only to find that your spouse and all your possessions are nowhere in sight. Someone even moved the condo where you are staying! We all know what happened. The current carried you down the shoreline. You became distracted with talking or playing, then without realizing it, you drifted.

Many times our marriages float down the shore because we have become distracted. We drift away from working together as a team and become individual silos. We're no longer enjoying an intimate friendship. "Mission Drift unfolds slowly. Like a current, it carries our marriages and families away from their core purpose and identity."[2]

What happens when you drift from your mission but still have a good marriage? Maybe you and your spouse are getting along well and enjoying life. Often, when we drift from our mission, the issue isn't what the marriage is; the problem is what the marriage is not. It's possible to have a healthy relationship that looks nothing like our purpose. We aren't acting according to who God created us to be. Our marriage might be good, but it serves no good purpose for the world around us when we become wrapped up in creating "our little world." We can be in a happy marriage without fulfilling our purpose. But happiness is too small a goal to warrant the death, burial, and resurrection of Christ. We must stay on mission!

Avoiding the Drift

When our family goes camping, one of our favorite things is cooking out (and eating)! The twin-burner, propane-fueled camping stove is about twenty-five years old and is as reliable as it gets for outdoor meal prep. However, food doesn't cook very well when there's no flame. Since our little green stove is so dependable, that usually only happens when one of the gas-filled cylinders runs out of propane. When we realize the flame has gone out, we just reach into our camping "stash" and grab a new one so we can re-apply the heat and get back to cooking (which results in eating!)

As with cooking, if you remove the heat from your mission, it will naturally begin to cool. When you realize this has happened, you must "re-apply the heat" to make sure you don't drift. What we see in science we found to be the norm within marriages. "Here's the reality: Mission Drift is the natural course, and it takes focused attention to safeguard against it. Once you ignore its source of heat, drift is only a matter of time."[3]

Staying on course and avoiding the "drift" is a daily battle, and you must fight against it. I am a pastoral counselor, but my position on staff at my church is that of Executive Pastor. I know it's an odd combination. As Executive Pastor, my job is to work with our ministry staff and team leaders to maintain our culture and keep our teams on the mission we believe God has set before us. Avoiding the drift is so essential that our church has a dedicated person on staff to fight against it.

There are inevitably times we notice that a team member isn't aligning with our staff culture or drifting from our mission. My job is to work with that person to guide them back to our staff culture and help them get back on track. More often than not, this process works wonderfully. Like going to the chiropractor, a simple adjustment or conversation is all it takes. We all need that occasionally.

However, there are other times that it is more like intense surgery. After many meetings, conversations, and 90-day "realignment" plans, we may realize this person is no longer a culture fit or can't help us achieve our ministry objective. Every once in a while, the individual agrees with us and quietly moves on. Sometimes they don't. At that point, I consult with our senior leadership team, and we decide how to cut ties with them. Yes, they get fired... at a church. I know, it does seem unkind. But two things are more unkind; allowing someone to sit within an organization they don't fit with when they could be thriving in a different one and allowing that person to keep your organization from accomplishing its mission.

Usually, when I have to "let someone go," their feelings toward me are no longer pleasant. I have lost many close friends through this process, and it was personally painful. Was it worth it? Yes. When I look at our staff and see them back on track in a healthy culture, it makes it all worthwhile.

"Firing" things from your life may be necessary for you to stay on mission and avoid the drift with your family. No, don't fire your spouse. However, there will be activities and even people you will need to move out of your family's life. These activities or people may not be inherently bad; they just don't propel you in the direction God is taking you. Learning to say "no," is tough, but when you see what God desires to do in and through your marriage and family, it's all worth it!

When Mission Eclipses Connection

"F-9." "Miss." "G-5," "Hit!" The tension was mounting. I had dedicated time and energy to this and was about to lose it all! The almost middle school girl sitting in front of me showed no mercy as she sat behind her small travel-sized game of Battleship, barking out commands. Taylor Swift was blasting through the sound bar. Bonnie was driving, with Colby navigating from an old paper roadmap (he loves roadmaps).

As I sat taking in that moment, not to sound trite, but time stood still. There in that old RV driving across windy Oklahoma, the purpose of the entire trip was realized. I thought to myself, *I don't think the Grand Canyon can eclipse this moment.* If this were a movie, this would be shot with creative angles, in slow motion, capturing Josie's beautiful smile as Louis Armstrong sings *What a Wonderful World.* And, of course, Chris Hemsworth would play my character. That was the moment when I truly understood the statement that opens every one of our podcast episodes, "Welcome to the Marriage Adventure Podcast, *where the journey is the destination*!" If that's true, I had reached my chosen destination.

We truly believe God has a grand mission for your marriage. He wants you to experience the fullness of an adventurous marriage relationship and enjoy each other as you shine a light for Jesus. If you are a goal-oriented person, this book's message is likely to resonate with you, driving you to lead your family to discover your purpose and identify smaller missions to work toward. But, let us issue a word of caution. As vital as it is to have a vision for where your marriage is going, don't allow your mission to eclipse your connection.

A year and a half ago, God began to write a vision on our hearts for a ministry. We felt compelled to provide resources to encourage husbands and wives to keep their finger on the pulse of their relationship. Remember the breakfast we had that was our "THAT'S ENOUGH" moment? We left our broken-hearted friends with a fire in our bellies to do something, anything we could, to fortify marriages against the assault of the enemy. Eight months later, we launched The Marriage Adventure Podcast.

While praying through what a ministry to couples would look like, we had many conversations about how it would affect our marriage. From the first month we started dating, we began ministering together. I immediately joined Daniel in ministering to the handful of students at the little mission church where he was Minister of Music and Youth. A year after we were married, we graduated from college and began traveling all over the southeastern United States, leading worship and working with student praise bands through our little non-profit ministry called WorshipOne.

Daniel and I continued to work side-by-side when we came on staff part-time at NorthStar Church to develop the middle and high school worship bands. It was a bittersweet day when we shut down our ministry for Daniel to accept a full-time position as Worship Pastor. Thirteen years later, he moved into the role of Executive Pastor and I came home to invest in our children.

God had taught us so many lessons through our twenty-five years of ministry together. So, when we began to pray about launching another parachurch ministry, I had a flashback to one of the most challenging seasons of our marriage. God led us to shut down WorshipOne at the height of our conference days. It was an easy decision for me. Although we worked well together to run a business that was reaching many people, I was not happy.

We were running as fast as we could toward our mission. The fast pace and forward progress kept Daniel invigorated. He is best when he has a lot on his plate and stays busy, but I was feeling left behind; not in ministry, not as Daniel's business partner, but as his wife. So, as much as I desired to help other couples through their marriage adventure, I wanted assurance that we wouldn't return to merely being business partners.

Men, track with me on this. If you are walking with Jesus, your wife will most likely follow wherever you lead her. But, if you don't keep a heart connection with her, you will see the light go out in her eyes. Do not allow the pursuit of a better job, a bigger house, important connections, your child's future, or even ministry to overshadow intimate friendship with your wife.

Women, we aren't exempt from our own pitfalls. Though we tend to be more relational than men, we can also allow our passions to overtake us and derail our relationship with our husbands. Many marriages get sacrificed on the altar of child-rearing. We begin the journey of parenthood with a common goal of loving and raising little people together. But if we aren't careful, all of our attention and affection can be poured out on the children, pushing our husband out in the cold. Guard your affections, even against giving them all away to your babies.

Every family dynamic is different. Maybe you both enjoy full-time jobs and share the responsibilities at home. You may be in full-time ministry at your church. You may homeschool your children with the mission of releasing godly, self-sustained, contributing adults into the world when they graduate from high school. Your family may be model missionaries to your co-workers, athletic teams, and communities. However, if you have successfully reached a common mission but have not invested in meaningful connections with your spouse, you could end up as strangers. Make sure you are taking time to enjoy the trip along the way. Your journey is part of your destination.

What about Personal Goals?

We believe God has called us to a mission as a married couple and as a family. We work together to show God's love to those around us. But does that leave any room for personal goals and missions?

We all have different personality styles. Sometimes we're born with a particular personality; sometimes, life shapes it for us. I'm the youngest of four boys. Typically, the youngest is thought to be spoiled, not driven but lazy... you get the picture. However, I'm not that way. I'm not sure if I was born that way or shaped into it out of my desire to not be thought of as a "typical youngest." On the Enneagram Personality Test, I'm a Type Three, which is an Achiever. I am a goal setter. If I don't have a goal to reach or a project to work on, I am not in a good place. Being a driven person is all fine until you get married!

The year our oldest child turned one, I decided to sign up and do an Olympic distance triathlon. I trained hard and completed the race. That was my goal- to finish. After the race, I looked to Bonnie and said, "Ya know, I'm halfway to a Half-Ironman?" The comment wasn't as much of a statement as it was a question. Bonnie looked at me and said," Um, we need to talk."

Men, you know it's never good when your wife says that! Personal goal setting was fine when we didn't have children. But now that we had a toddler, my personal goals were stealing time and money from my family. Not to mention the safety issue of biking on a busy highway. This situation forced me to ask myself, "Is my type 'A' personality and my drive to reach new goals hurting my relationship with my wife?"

After a lot of soul searching and talking with Bonnie, I realized that I needed to slow my appetite for achievement. So I did. Slowing down was great for Bonnie and the kids. They had more of me and more of my attention. However, I began to realize that after a while, it was killing me. Not having a bulls-eye on the wall was stripping me of the person God created me to be. I am a much better person, father, and husband when I am achieving and moving forward. I had to go back to the drawing board and continue soul searching. "God, how can I balance who you made me to be with the person my family *needs* me to be?" After much prayer and over a few years, God showed me how to balance this.

> Listen to *The Marriage Adventure Podcast, Episode 31* to find out how to balance personal goal setting and family time. www.themarriageadventure.com/podcasts

We realized that when I can utilize my goal setting and drive to move my family forward, it's better for everyone. It can inspire my wife and children to set goals and achieve them. It's good for them to see Daddy doing something challenging and finishing it, so they are willing to do the same. However, I had to realize that everyone doesn't move at the pace I like to run. Instead of encouraging my family forward, I was bulldozing them, which eventually created resentment. I needed to slow down and encourage them along, not drag them forward. I also had to open my eyes and inspire them to dream *their* dreams, then help them accomplish them.

There's nothing wrong with having personal dreams. They can keep you invigorated. I still wanted to achieve and set personal goals, but I had to learn to do it in a healthy way. If a personal goal drains my family's bank account... it's not healthy. If it steals precious time away from my children and my wife... it's not healthy. I had to find ways to take some time for myself that didn't leave my family wondering, *where's Daddy?*

Going back to school to work on my Master's degree was a challenge at keeping balance. I included Bonnie in the process, and we prayed about it together before I took it on. It made it an "us" goal instead of a "me" goal. Bonnie felt that she'd rather me take a lighter load each semester instead of loading up on classes to finish quickly. That way, I would still time for them. Also, I got up at 5:00 every morning and did my school work while everyone slept. That way, I could be with my family after work until bedtime. Just these simple things helped keep balance in my life.

If you are a type "A" personality like me, God created you that way for a reason. However, we have to realize that unless we bring our drive and goal setting into a balance, it can destroy our marriage. My new goal is for Bonnie to love my dreams instead of resenting them because they make me a better husband. Personal goals can be healthy. Just don't allow them to create conflict in your marriage that ultimately distracts you from your family's mission.

Knowing where you are going and dreaming together about how to get there is important. But, if you don't stay connected to each other as you work toward your goals, you may find your marriage adrift. If you drive hard across the country for days to reach the Grand Canyon, but get there to find your spouse didn't get back in the car with you somewhere along the way, was the trip worth it? On this marriage adventure, the journey is as important as the destination. Make sure you are enjoying all the scenic views along the way.

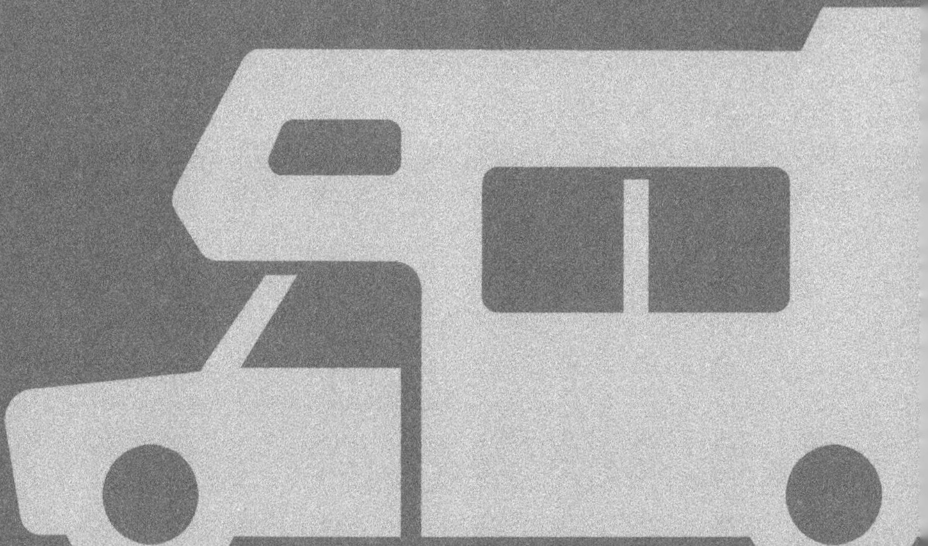

CHAPTER 14:

READY, SET, GO!

"Remember when we got so far up the side of Bell Rock that I almost cried?"

Traveling I-40 at sunset, with Sedona two days in our rear-view mirror, I imagined a grown-up Josie fifteen years in the future, sitting across the table from her brother at a Thanksgiving dinner. I smile, envisioning their laughter and telling our grandchildren stories about this Hoover Super Trip that begin with, "remember when...."

"Yeah! Remember how we held our breath every time we crossed a state line, and we got thirty-three truckers to honk their horns at us? And how Daddy wouldn't answer us for a whole day unless we called him 'Papa' like on Little House on the Prairie!" Colby responds.

"That's right! And remember how we crossed the creek at Crescent Moon Ranch without Mama and Daddy and couldn't get back across! And Charlie-dog played in the snow for the first time! Don't forget watching ten hours of Little House on the Prairie because it was the only DVDs we had in the motorhome. And when you ate chocolate cake EVERY night!" The more Josie reaches back to her childhood, the more Colby remembers.

"That was the first time we ever heard Johnny Cash. I still have the flattened pennies from every stop we made! Those were good times," Colby smiles.

With only a day of driving left until we reached home, I reflected on all we had experienced on our two-week trip. I was beyond exhausted, ready to pull into our driveway, but had an overwhelming feeling of happiness settle over me. We had done it! With all the challenges, cancellations, last-minute campsite reservations, missed turns, and unexpected detours, we were still intact. Better than that, we had taken a trip that we had been dreaming of. It hadn't been perfect. But it was spectacular!!

Rear View Mirror

Whether it was fifty days or fifty years ago, when you stood at an altar as bright-eyed lovers, with the open road of possibility before you, what did you have in mind? With dreams of excitement, romance, and happily ever after, few couples begin their marriage adventure with a clear vision of what it takes to reach the finish line.

My (Daniel) parents have been married for 60 years. Throughout their marriage adventure, they have both fellowshipped with Christ, had many common missions, and worked together as a team raising four boys. But you don't make a marriage last 60 years without an intimate friendship.

Recently, I drove them to Nashville, TN, to an eye doctor appointment. My 85-year-old dad recently lost almost all of his vision due to macular degeneration. They were hoping that this specialist could help fit him in some glasses that would allow him to see. They were so hopeful. The night before the appointment, in the hotel room, I overheard them as they were excitedly making plans for what they would do once Dad could see better. They anticipated a miracle. It was as if they were two teenagers dreaming and making plans. While the doctor ran several tests on my dad's vision, we sat in the examination room.

As the exam progressed, Mom and I could see that the look on the doctor's face was not hopeful. I reached over and grabbed my mom's hand as her eyes filled with tears, then ran down her cheek. In an instant, I knew that their desires for one last dash of adventures in their next few years together wouldn't work out as they had dreamed.

As tears welled up in my eyes, I sat there thinking to myself, *What a strange world we live in. What I'm seeing happen between my mom and dad is the culmination of the dream. This is why you get married when you are young; so, one day, when you are old and gray, blind and broken, you can end your adventure together.*

My mom and dad recently celebrated their sixtieth wedding anniversary. They reminisce a lot these days, mostly about the good times. Dad's military career moved them ten times in twenty years. They raised four godly boys who married wonderful Godly women. They beam just thinking of their ten grandchildren. All these years later, they still call each other "Dear" and "Honey." When they sit on the couch, they always hold hands. When they lie in bed, they still spoon each other.

But their journey wasn't all mountain tops. Mom and Dad experienced their share of rocky roads and heartaches. They walked through infertility and miscarriages and survived the teenage years of four boys. They cared for each other through sickness and held each other up when they lost aging parents, siblings, and friends.

When viewing their lifelong adventure through the rearview mirror, my parents have a perspective that they didn't in their newlywed twenties. They now have the experience to know that their detours didn't define them. Their valleys led to paths that eventually moved them to scenic heights.

Listen to *The Marriage Adventure Podcast*, Episode 51 to hear an interview with Daniel's parents on their 60th wedding anniversary. www.themarriageadventure.com/podcasts

That's the beauty of "til death do us part." Every day won't be sunshine and seaside hammocks. Nor will they all be defined by desperately clinging to the side of Bell Rock. On this side of the peaks and troughs, two things have remained constant in my parents' sixty-year journey, their pursuit of Christ and each other.

But this book is about your marriage adventure. When your journey is coming to an end, what do you want to see in your rearview mirror? What hopes and dreams do you have for your relationship? Deep down, do you sense that God has drawn you and your spouse together for a purpose bigger than fifty years of muddling through the mundane?

Have you ever looked up Google Earth online and typed in your address? If you've never done this, you should try it just for fun. The page opens with a satellite view of our globe from space. Then, when you enter a location, it zooms in, dropping you practically on your front doorstep. It's an eerie feeling knowing a camera so far away can inspect your activities by the click of a button. But that's another story! Now pull back from your location all the way to where you started.

Something amazing happens when you can see a 10,000-foot drone view of your lives. You see yourself in light of the bigger picture. God can see your entire journey, with the beginning and destination in the same glance. He knows the plans He has for your life and marriage, and they are bigger than the argument you had over breakfast. They are more fulfilling than the house and vacation you are pouring all your effort into saving for. The scope of His calling is grander than which pre-school or college your children will attend. It's even more marvelous than your idea of "happily ever after."

When we allow the "in the beginning" God to reveal His mission for our marriage, suddenly our relationship is infused with meaning. When we learn to walk in step with Christ daily, serve each other, and use our unique gifts to move toward a common mission, it becomes easier to release the things that don't matter. We begin to see our spouse as our teammate rather than our enemy. And it gives us renewed strength and an intimate friendship to face our adventure together.

Making Progress

Do you remember the couple who began this journey with us broken down on the side of the road? Matt's and Millie's issue wasn't a lack of love for one another. They had plenty of that. Matt's and Millie's problem was that they started filling their life with a lot of stuff before they knew what they wanted to do with it. They essentially jumped in the car and started driving but never asked or answered the question of where they were going.

After they came to see me, we began looking at their spiritual life and mapping a mission and vision for their family based upon God's design. Discovering God's greater plan for their marriage allowed them to prioritize life and all they had in it.

Soon after, we looked at Matt's and Millie's ability to work as a team. We assessed their individual strengths and weaknesses, which gave them a deeper understanding of each other. Once this began taking shape, they noticed their friendship deepening. By prioritizing adventures and date nights, their intimacy grew. Matt and Millie are working hard to stay on their mission. It's a process, but now they are doing it together.

Ready...

When our son was four, he was learning to get dressed all by himself. He was so proud one Sunday morning when he walked into the kitchen dressed from head to toe without the help of his Mama. We couldn't help but grin at his unlevel shirttail, recognizing he was off by one button-hole all the way down. As we bragged about how grown up he was, he didn't even notice my swift rebuttoning job.

Colby did his best four-year-old job of putting himself together that morning. He had brushed his teeth, slicked down his hair, and managed to get dressed. However, our independent buddy made one critical mistake. He missed the top button.

Our relationship with Christ is the top-button issue. We can have the best intentions for the race we are running. We can plot a course for our marriage and even accomplish a few good things. Still, without the internal compass of connection with God, we won't fully realize the grand mission God has created us for! If we miss the top button, everything else will be out of alignment.

Are you ready to experience all God has in store for your marriage? If so, where do you start? With the top button. Maybe you have never considered doing anything with the person of Jesus Christ. Do you know that you belong to Him? The Bible says that if we do nothing with Jesus, we have chosen to reject Him. God is perfect and cannot have a relationship with us based on our own works because there is nothing we could ever do to measure up to His holiness. Remember what happened in the Garden of Eden? Our fellowship was broken. But God sent Jesus to rescue us. A relationship with Him is the only way to get to heaven (John 14:6).

If you want to enter into the restored fellowship that is available through God's Son, Jesus Christ, we invite you to take that step! Understand that everyone sins, and no one is perfect like God (Romans 3:23). If we don't turn away from our sin, the punishment we earn is death and separation from God (Romans 6:23).

But, God loves us too much not to give us an option for salvation. He sent His own perfect Son, Jesus, to take punishment in our place (John 3:16). To receive God's forgiveness, we just believe in Jesus' life, His death on the cross, and His resurrection, and confess that we need Him to save us from our sins (1 John 1:9, Romans 10:9). When this takes place in our hearts, our adoption into God's family is complete!

There is nothing else you are required to do to be saved. But, before you begin mapping a mission for your marriage, it is wise to be growing in your faith so you can hear clearly from Jesus. The closer you walk with Him, the more likely you will be to hear His voice. Your mission will flow out of connection with Him. Healthy marriages begin with healthy individuals who are walking in fellowship with Christ daily. (You will find an appendix in the back of the book to offer further guidance on growing in your relationship with Christ).

Set...

Are you ready to map out a mission for your marriage? Have you discovered how God wants to use your combined strengths to impact people around you for His Kingdom? We challenge you to follow the guidelines in Chapters 3 and 4 to help you discover your unique mission. Yours is not the same as ours because every couple has a different calling.

Maybe the two of you will lead couples groups at your church and show other husbands and wives what it looks like to love each other sacrificially. Perhaps your daily investment in your children will produce little world-changers who influence their friends to love Jesus. Maybe your whole family will become a beacon of light in every extra-curricular activity you participate in.

Of course, there will be bumps in the road, and you'll have to course-correct yearly. But, finding your mission and writing down your core values will give you a destination and road map to keep you from wandering aimlessly through this crazy broken world. There has never been a time that the world needs to see hope and light through your marriage more than now!

Go!

Very few people start their marriage journey with the expectation that they will become bitter enemies. They start down the same path, united in their destination of happily ever after, bound together by their intimate friendship. They sit side-by-side in the driver and passenger seats, envisioning their best adventures ahead.

Your dreams can become a reality if you are both willing to keep your eyes on the road, celebrate the most brilliant views along the way, look for the best in each other, extend grace through every detour, and stay vigilant in your awareness of the snares set to deter you.

God has a purpose for your marriage far greater than fifty years of highs and lows. His design for your marriage is the same as the very first one He created. Though our setting is no longer Paradise, God wants to live His life through you. When He does, this will enable you to love each other in such a way that your family, friends, and neighbors see something different... the picture of His great love for them. He wants to bind your hearts together in a sacred union and commission you to accomplish more for His glory than you ever could apart.

This journey is more than just not being alone. You have the opportunity to join your hearts in an intimate friendship that gives you a taste of the fulfillment God offers through a relationship with His son, Jesus Christ. Now, it's your turn. Go! Be fruitful and multiply. Your Marriage Adventure starts now!

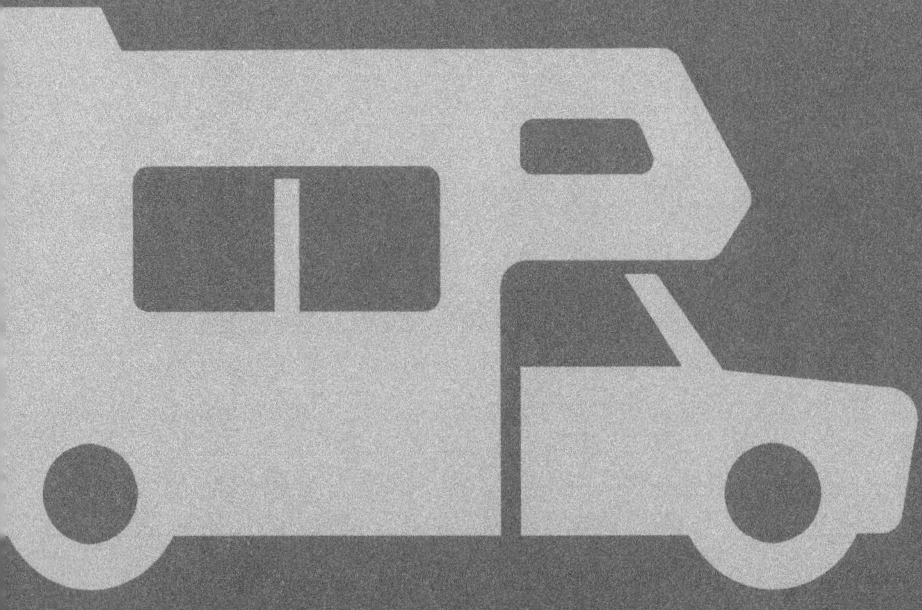

APPENDIX

GROWING IN CHRIST

Our daughter, Josie, is a true artist. She loves to create through music, drama, art, and, most recently, videography. She spent quite a bit of money she had saved from birthdays and holidays to invest in a GoPro camera. Our family planned to head out for a weekend adventure, and Josie wanted to bring her GoPro camera along. She became frustrated when her battery kept dying, and she couldn't get it to hold a charge.

That's when inspiration hit her, and Josie asked if she could borrow the power inverter we use in the car. See, the power inverter she's talking about plugs into our 12-volt power in the vehicle and converts it to a 110 outlet. That way, we can plug in our computers and charge our phones while driving. Josie said, "If I can put that in my backpack, I can keep my camera battery charged all the time." While that sounded great, Josie didn't understand that the power inverter has to be plugged into an actual power source to charge her battery. It doesn't produce power on its own. It merely converts it to a usable form of power.

The same is true in our marriage. We can be kind for a while until our "kindness" battery runs out. Patience will keep us on track for a season, even if our joy is gone. We can't produce power on our own.

We can only stay charged by our connection to the Holy Spirit. He will empower us to love our spouse the way God desires for us to love them.

In John 15:5, Jesus gives us the answer to keeping our connection with Him. He said, "I am the vine; you are the branches. Whoever abides in me and I in him, he it is that bears much fruit, for apart from me, you can do nothing." Did you catch it? He who abides in me bears much fruit. We abide in Him. The scripture goes on to say in verses 9-13:

> As the Father has loved me, so have I loved you. Abide in my love. If you keep my commandments, you will abide in my love, just as I have kept my Father's commandments and abide in his love. These things I have spoken to you, that my joy may be in you, and that your joy may be full. This is my commandment, that you love one another as I have loved you. Greater love has no one than this, that someone lay down his life for his friends (John 15:9-13).

Every time we tell couples that the key to their marriage is found through fellowship or an abiding relationship with Christ, they want to know, "How? How do we abide?" What does that even mean? Abide sounds like such a big, old-fashioned, unattainable word. Let us simplify it. To abide means: 1) to remain; continue; stay; 2) to have one's abode; dwell; reside; 3) to continue in a particular condition, attitude, relationship.[1]

The idea of abiding in Christ is nothing more than staying in fellowship with Him and continuing to walk with Him. *Great! But what do I DO?* The act of abiding doesn't mean that you strive to do anything; it's more about surrendering. Andrew Murray explains it this way in his book *Abide in Christ*:

> Abiding in Him is not a work that we have to do as a condition for enjoying His salvation, but a consenting to let Him do all for us, and in us, and through us. It is a work He does for us-- the fruit and the power of His redeeming love. Our part is simply to yield, trust, and wait for what He has engaged to perform.[2]

Recently, I (Daniel) was given a great example of what it means to abide. When we began writing this book, Christmas was approaching, and we had decided that rather than giving our kids a bunch of presents, we were going to purchase season passes to Six Flags Theme Park. I bought them online, but I had to physically go to the park before the deadline to get free parking and some other goodies. So, while the kids finished putting up Christmas decorations, I snuck out and drove over to the park and got what I needed.

While inside the park, I got to thinking, *I'm here. I might as well have a few minutes of fun!* So, I did what any grown man inside a theme park by himself would do; I walked over to the Mind Bender roller coaster and got in line. Keep in mind; it's been years since I've been on a coaster! As I sat in the seat, I didn't even think twice. The ride attendant secured the lap bar, and I was soon on my way up the first big hill. Midway up, I started thinking, (it's never good to overthink when riding a coaster,) *Wow, this is a big hill. I hope I don't lose my glasses. Wow, this is a big, big hill!*

Speeding down that first hill, I threw my hands in the air, determined to keep them up. As we went into the first loop, my neck and head were pulling back, and I struggled to keep my hands raised. There's something about the centrifugal force that works against keeping your hands raised on a roller coaster. At that moment, I did something. I just relaxed. I gave into the coaster. I leaned my head back, held onto the bar in front of me, and enjoyed the ride. I began to abide. As the ride ended and I was getting off, I thought to myself, *that was awesome!* I felt like a kid again. By the way, I did lose my glasses.

Riding a roller coaster is an amazing picture of what it means to abide. We accept our position in Christ, sit secured by the lap belt of God's truth, then move where He moves us. When we climb the hills of the coaster, we are secure in Him. When we nearly faint through plummets of life, He holds us. Rather than striving to hold ourselves in the coaster or go our own way, we relax into the work that was done on the cross and allow Him to continue to shape us on the journey. This resting doesn't typically come naturally to us, so we look for things we can do out of our effort.

For all of you who struggle to simply acquiesce, you'll be relieved to know that there are some things you can *do* in that state of surrender and waiting. Just understand, you will be as frustrated and tired as I was trying to raise my hands on the roller coaster if you are replacing God's work through you with your own work in these areas.

When we abide in the love of Christ, His fruit will come out. When we remain in Him, Jesus is the one who completes our joy. It's not dependent on our spouse. When we let Him work through us, we are strengthened to love each other as He has loved us, with a willingness to lay our lives down for our spouse. This is real love. Jesus said there's no greater love on earth. It starts with abiding.

How to Abide

Abiding in Christ is a spiritual positioning of recognizing who you are *in* Christ. But you can also physically position yourself in a place to hear from the Lord on an ongoing basis. You can surround yourself with godly people in a local church body and begin filling your mind with good things. We like to filter what we allow to come into our lives and minds through Philippians 4:8. "Finally, brothers and sisters, whatever is true, whatever is noble, whatever is right, whatever is pure, whatever is lovely, whatever is admirable—if anything is excellent or praiseworthy—think about such things."

Filling our minds with godly teaching, music, and content is a great way to open ourselves up to hearing from the Holy Spirit. The clearer our minds are of the things that would distract us from the Lord, the better chance we have to hear from Him and walk with Him daily.

As encouraging as it is to listen to teachers from the local church, the most direct place to hear from the Lord is through reading His word for yourself. God inspired the Bible as a way for us to hear from His heart. Through Bible study, we engage our minds with truth that hasn't changed since the Holy Spirit breathed it. Then the Holy Spirit living inside us makes God's words connect with us in a way that it never did before salvation.

We both love connecting with others in Bible studies, but God wants to speak to each of us personally through his word. He loves to reveal Himself to every one of His children individually. He tells us in Jeremiah 29:13, "You will seek me and find me, when you seek me with all your heart." God isn't hiding from us and has revealed Himself through the scriptures. It's amazing how the scriptures come alive and are fresh for every season. A verse you read as a child can breathe life into you an entirely new way twenty years later in your time of greatest need.

If you've never read the Bible on your own, it might sound intimidating. But it can be as simple as **READ**ing it. This easy acrostic may help you get started.

Read the passage in context. Who wrote it? To whom was it written? What was the universal lesson or truth in the verses?

Evaluate how the passage speaks into your life, attitude, or current circumstance?

Ask the Lord how he wants you to respond to what you read.

Do what he impressed on your heart.

We understand that it's a big Book! You may be wondering, *even if I **READ** it, where do I start?* If you aren't following a particular reading plan or study, we recommend trying this order.

1. John- John walks through the life of Jesus and His purpose for coming to earth.
2. Acts- Picks up with how the first believers began living as the Church and shows the spread of the news of Jesus as Savior.
3. 1 John, 2 John- These books stress the love of God and how to follow Jesus' example of loving others.
4. Psalms- These are written as songs or poems. They are very expressive of the writers' emotions and easy to identify with.
5. Proverbs- Short, practical tidbits of advice from the wisest man to ever live.
6. Any of the New Testament Epistles. That's just a big word for letters written to churches. For

example, Paul wrote the book of Galatians to the church in Galatia.

Not only does God want to share His heart with you, but He also wants you to share yours with Him. The fancy word for that is "prayer," but it's just talking to God. He tells us in 1 Peter 5:7 to "Cast all your anxiety on him because He cares for you." He wants you to tell him all the things that worry you and make your heart heavy. 1 Thessalonians 5:16-18 says it this way, "Rejoice always, pray continually, give thanks in all circumstances; for this is God's will for you in Christ Jesus." He's pretty much asking you to tell Him about all the things that make you happy. Tell Him about them all the time and give Him thanks in every circumstance, even the bad ones. He wants to be in an ongoing conversation with you.

When we come to know God's heart through His word and spend time talking to Him every day, a transformation begins to happen inside us. We start looking more like Jesus and begin to learn what He likes and doesn't like. We are "transformed by the renewing of [our] minds and can test and approve what God's will is" (Rom. 12:2). Abiding in Christ boils down to this, "Delight yourself in the Lord, and He will give you the desires of your heart" (Ps. 37:4). When He puts His desires in your heart, His desires become yours; His heart and love for people becomes yours, His desire to love and serve your spouse becomes yours, and the Holy Spirit inside you gives you the power to love the way Jesus loves. There is no greater love! "Greater love has no one than this, that someone lay down his life for his friends" (John 15:13).

With my eyes fixed on Jesus instead of myself, dependent on Him to meet my needs, His love, joy, peace, patience, etc., works out of me to serve my spouse. This is a sacrificial, self-less, real love sustained by the Holy Spirit living inside of me! If you're starting to think, *Well, that's great for my spouse, but is there any fulfillment in it for me?* Christ gives us hope for what can happen when we obey and let Him work through us. Jesus says, "These things I have spoken to you, that my joy may be in you, and that your joy may be full" (John 15:11). He tells us that His joy will be in us, and our joy will be FULL. This isn't just a formula for some out of reach or fleeting happiness. This is a lasting joy that overflows. This joy moves marriages onto an entirely higher plane.

NOTES

Introduction

1. Juliana Menasce, Nikki Graf, and Gretchen. "Marriage and Cohabitation in the U.S." *Pew Research,* 6 November 2019, https://www.pewresearch.org/social-trends/2019/11/06/marriage-and-cohabitation-in-the-u-s/; Geiger, A.W. and Gretchen Livingston. "8 Facts about Love and Marriage in America." *Pew Research, 13* February 2019, https://www.pewresearch.org/fact-tank/2019/02/13/8-facts-about-love-and-marriage/; Luscombe, Belinda. "The Divorce Rate is Dropping." *Time,* Time USA, LLC, 26 November 2018, https://time.com/5434949/divorce-rate-children-marriage-benefits/; "Trends Redefining Romance Today," *Barna*, Barna Group, 9 February 2017, https://www.barna.com/research/trends-redefining-romance-today/

Chapter 1

1. Mark Batterson, *Play the Man* (Grand Rapids, MI: Baker Books, 2017), 127.

Chapter 2

1. John Piper, "The Image of God, an Approach from Biblical and Systematic Theology," *desiringGod,* (March,1st 1971): https://www.desiringgod.org/articles/the-image-of-god.

2. Matt Perman, *What's Best Next* (Grand Rapids, MI: Zondervan 2016), 151.

3. Rick Warren, *Purpose Driven Life* (Grand Rapids, MI: Zondervan, 2002), 18.

4. Perman, p.154.

Chapter 3
1. Stephen Covey, *The 7 Habits of Highly Effective Families* (New York, NY, Macmillan, 2014), p. 88.

2. Debbie Stocker, "Vision, values, and purpose according to Collins and Porras", Stocker Partnership: https://www.stockerpartnership.com/resources/articles/vision-values-and-purpose-according-to-collins-and-porras/.

Chapter 4
1. George Barna, *The Power of Vision, Third Edition* (Grand Rapids, MI: Baker Books, 1992), 28.

2. Ibid, 40.

3. Ibid, 41.

Chapter 6
1. Jack Hibbs, "When God Gets A Hold of Your Marriage, Part 1." Sermon, Calvary Chapel, Chino Hills, September 16th, 2018.

2. Ibid.

3. Ibid.

Chapter 7
1. John and Staci Eldridge, *Captivating: Unveiling the Mystery of a Woman's Soul* (Nashville, TN: Thomas Nelson, April 17, 2011), 32.

2. Dorothy Patterson, Ph.D., *The Woman's Role in Marriage* (Dr. James Dobson's Family Talk, August 12, 2013).

3. Patterson, Ibid.

Chapter 9

1. Pat Summit, *Quotes from the Summit* (Pat Summit Leadership Group, A Member of Southwestern Family of Companies/Premium Press America, 2019, Print.

2. Ibid.

3. Dr. Eric Scalise "10 Rules in Creating a Win-Win Marriage," ieyenews.com, From Dr. James Dobson's family talk, October 28th, 2018.

Chapter 10

1. C.S. Lewis, *The Four Loves* (New York, NY: Harper Collins Publishers, 1960. Originally published in 1960 by Harcourt Brace) 82, https://read.amazon.com/?asin=B01EFM8NI4.

2. Gary Chapman, *The 5 Love Languages* (Chicago, IL: Northfield Publishing, 1992), 33.

3. Dr. Tim and Darcy Kimmel, *Grace Filled Marriage* (Franklin, TN: Worthy Books, 2013), 11.

Chapter 11

1. Gottman John and Nan Silver. *The Seven Principles for Making Marriage Work*, (New York NY: Three Rivers Press, 1999), 17.

2. Louie Giglio, "How Great is Our God," Passion Talk Series. (Capitol Christian Distribution, Six Steps Records, 2009).

3. Van Edwards, Vanessa. "The (Surprising) Science of Orgasms." Science of People. https://www.scienceofpeople.com/science-orgasms/.

4. John Eldridge, *Wild at Heart* (Nashville, TN: Thomas Nelson, Nashville, TN, 2010); John and Staci Eldridge, *Captivating: Unveiling the Mystery of a Woman's Soul* (Nahsville, TN: Thomas Nelson, April 17, 2011).

5. Nicole Galas, "Does Sex Provide Health Benefit? Medical News Today, Medically reviewed by Jane Brito, Ph.D., LCSW, CST on August 23, 2019. © 2004-2020 Healthline Media UK Ltd, Brighton, UK, a Red Ventures Company. https://www.medical-newstoday.com/articles/316954.php

Chapter 13
1. Peter Greer and Chris Horst, *Mission Drift* (Minneapolis, MN: Bethany House Publishers, 2014, 15.

2. Ibid,18.

3. Ibid, 20.

Appendix
Growing in Christ
1. Dictionary.com unabridged based on The Random House Unabridged Dictionary, copyright Random House, Inc. 2021, https://www.dictionary.com/browse/abide?s=t.

2. Murray, Andrew. *Abide in Christ* (New Kensington, PA: Whitaker House, 1979), 28.

ABOUT THE AUTHORS

We're Daniel & Bonnie Hoover, and one of our greatest joys is tackling this adventure of life, family, and ministry together as intimate friends! After years of walking with couples through their most difficult seasons of marriage, we've seen that the enemy has launched an assault on the core of the church–marriages and the family. Our hearts have been broken, and God has given us a massive calling to help couples develop a healthy biblical marriage. Our prayer is that you will join us on this journey of the highs, the lows, and everything in between, and you'll experience marriage as the adventure God has designed it to be.

We endured the heartache and miracle of infertility, then walked the road of adoption, and are now blessed to be the parents of Josie (11) and Colby (9). Bonnie has a BA in Psychology, and Daniel holds a Master's Degree in Pastoral Counseling and Leadership. Currently, we are both pursuing an advanced diploma in Marriage and Family.

While Daniel serves as Executive Pastor at NorthStar Church in Kennesaw, GA, he is also a pastoral counselor. He meets with couples daily to work through issues such as infidelity, infertility, communication, conflict resolution, poor financial management, parenting, etc. We are certified Prepare/Enrich facilitators, and together, we lead premarital workshops for couples preparing to be married and weekend intensive workshops for married couples.

Together, we host *The Marriage Adventure Weekly Podcast* and *The Marriage Adventure Blog*, where we discuss many topics that couples encounter on their marital journey. We also interview married couples ranging from authors and celebrities to pastors and their wives to the average everyday couple, who have endured extraordinary circumstances.

Listen on Spotify, Apple, & Google Play

Join Daniel & Bonnie Hoover every week for
The Marriage Adventure Podcast
where they discuss a multitude of topics that couples encounter on their marriage journey.

www.themarriageadventure.com

Follow us on Facebook & Instagram
@themarriageadventure

CPSIA information can be obtained
at www.ICGtesting.com
Printed in the USA
JSHW031345010421
13085JS00004B/15